CREW OF THREE

HOW BOLD DREAMS AND DETAILED PLANS LAUNCHED OUR FAMILY'S SAILING ADVENTURE

By

Kimberly J. Ward

Download the Audiobook Free

As a way to thank you for purchasing this paperback or eBook, I am giving you the Audiobook version of *Crew of Three: How Bold Dreams and Detailed Plans Launched Our Family's Sailing Adventures* at no cost. I even narrated it myself!

Please visit my website to get your free gift:

www.KimberlyJWardWriter.com/Audiobook

Crew of Three:
How Bold Dreams and Detailed Plans Launched Our
Family's Sailing Adventure

Requests to publish excerpts from this book, or media enquiries, should be
sent to: kward@iwillsustain.org

Paperback ISBN: 979-8-89109-102-3

EBook ISBN: 979-8-89109-103-0

Audiobook ISBN: 979-8-89109-182-5

Library of Congress Control Number: 2023914975

Published by KJW Publishing

Mattapoisett, MA

USA

Cover design: Jomel Pepito
Interior design: Heru Setiawan
Motif design: Cherí Ben-Iesau
Author Photo: Maggie Howland

www.KJWPublishing.com

For Michael and Ally,

without whom there would be no Crew of Three.

TABLE OF CONTENTS

"There are only two ways to live your life. One is as though nothing is a miracle. The other is as though everything is a miracle." —Albert Einstein

CHAPTER 1

THE PLAN

"Tell me, what is it you plan to do with your one wild and precious life?" —Mary Oliver

In July 2012, the sailing vessel *Field Trip* sailed into our cove, effectively changing the course of our lives.

What were we planning to do for the next decade? Likely, continue as we were. You know, the status quo. Though we generally choose trails off the beaten path, ours had become a comfortable, fairly ordinary suburban life. The only things missing were travel soccer and a minivan.

We loved to travel and had talked about taking a boat trip as a family. *Field Trip's* arrival signaled to my husband and me that it was time to seriously think it through. It was time to make a conscious decision to go sailing or not to go rather than let inertia keep us rooted. We decided at that moment to choose an unconventional life and to live authentically, by intention, not default. It was time to make a plan.

Always have a plan. And a Plan B. Maybe even C and D. Because though you can make plans, you can't plan the outcome. It is often said that sailors' plans are written in sand at low tide.

Also, make sure you have a sense of humor. You will definitely need a sense of humor. And coffee and wine. My husband would also add rum to the list.

I met Mark, *Field Trip's* captain, in 1995, when we both worked for Oracle. Over the years, Mark also got to know my husband, Michael, as we all worked in the same field. Yet, rather than the technical consulting we all did, they bonded over sailing. Before Michael and I met, he had taken two long sailing trips over the years: once to the Florida Keys aboard his sailboat, *Mad Hatter*, and the second to the Bahamas for the winter aboard his next sailboat, *Wayward*.

Mark confessed to Michael his dream was to sail around the world. He peppered Michael with question after question about his past trips. While Mark was fairly knowledgeable in a textbook kind of way, he had never really sailed. Michael pegged him as a "yammerer"—someone who talks a lot about something and never actually does it. And there are a lot of those out there. Besides, Mark was married to his work and the consulting lifestyle. He left Oracle and started his own firm, building it into a major player in the Oracle payroll world. We were sure he was eying a potential purchase by one of the big consulting companies and the partnership and money that would go along with that sort of transaction.

Imagine our surprise when, after he sold his company to one of the big firms, fulfilled his obligation to run the practice for an agreed amount of time, and reaped the financial rewards, he quit! During those years, he had married a lovely gal, moved to Colorado, and had two children. Also during those years, he and his wife had been busy gaining hands-on sailing skills by taking a variety of courses during every vacation. Did they have a plan? Indeed. So much for being a yammerer.

In 2011, Mark's family moved to an apartment in Argentina while their boat was being built. He was creative and hired a captain and crew when necessary and periodically flew his wife and kids to meet him and the boat until they were ready to sail alone as a family full time. The four of them made their first big passage aboard *Field Trip* from Bermuda to Newport, Rhode Island, and, in July 2012, sailed up to our mooring in Mattapoisett, Massachusetts.

As they had been at this "cruising thing" for much of a year, it was our turn to pepper them with questions. We thoroughly enjoyed our tour of *Field Trip*, their luxurious 44-foot Antares catamaran, a sailboat with two hulls, complete with a washing machine.

"I didn't even know that was an option," I marveled to my husband.

Michael, the realist, was quick to point out, for us, "It's not."

Michael has been sailing since he was a little boy and has owned boats his entire adult life. Big boats. Boats that require a truck to launch and haul—put in and take out of the water—and a crane to step—take down and set up—the mast. Mark was anxious to capitalize on Michael's vast experience, and we all set out aboard *Field Trip* for an overnight in Buzzards Bay. The guys flew her stunning spinnaker, the big colorful sail, for the first time and talked about diesel engines and anchoring and all things boats. Meanwhile, I got to know Mark's wife, Sarah, and started learning the ropes from her about homeschooling, small-space living, and managing a family aboard. Elizabeth and Michael, ages seven and five and already seasoned "boat kids," had instantly befriended our daughter, Ally, who was eight, and they were doing what kids do best: playing.

Over the next few days, I learned what makes a cruising gal happy: a full-size washer and dryer, a car to go shopping, girl time, and long showers. And then I learned what makes a cruiser—gal, guy, or kid—sad: saying "so long" to new, already dear friends.

I also learned that I loved the stability of a catamaran. Unlike a monohull, a catamaran is much more stable. With its two hulls, it barely heels, or leans over, while underway. Ever since Ally was born, I would, more frequently than not, get nauseous whenever we heeled. I was not able to go below to fix meals or to take care of anything else without getting seasick. While sailing on *Field Trip*, however, I did not have a problem.

The crew of *Field Trip* spent the next few weeks cruising up to Boston and through Maine and then came back to our cove before heading south to Florida and on to the Bahamas and the Eastern Caribbean. By the time we saw them again five weeks later, Michael and I had our own plan.

We have a passion for travel, so we've talked through dozens of adventures ever since we started dating in 2001. However, a trip on the boat had always been a nebulous "someday" kind of idea. How does a trip like that even work? Living on a boat, plans are primarily driven by the weather— hurricane season, prevailing winds, and currents. We talked in detail for the first time about what type of trip might be within reason for us.

We talked through a one-year trip, going down the East Coast from Massachusetts to Florida. From Florida, we would cross the Gulf Stream to the Bahamas, exploring a number of the 700 coral islands and 2,400 cays (pronounced "keys") that make up the island nation. And then, we would head back north to Massachusetts.

A two-year trip would look the same as the one-year trip to the Bahamas. Then, instead of retracing our steps north back home, we would head to Turks and Caicos and through the "Thorny Passage"—along the north coast of the Dominican Republic, through the Mona Passage, where the cold Atlantic meets the much warmer Caribbean, and along Puerto Rico's south coast. We would continue through the Virgins—Spanish, US, and British—to Saint Martin and then south through the Eastern Caribbean islands. After waiting out the hurricane season in Grenada, we would turn around and follow the same route back home.

"What about the Western Caribbean?"

"Can we go through the Panama Canal?"

"How do you go around the world in a sailboat anyway?"

I fired question after question at Michael, for which he mostly had ready answers. Of course, he has been reading about and studying all of this for years. He pulled out his well-worn copy of Jimmy Cornell's *World Cruising Routes: 1000 Sailing Routes in All of the Oceans* to illustrate many of his answers for me.

I was infatuated with the idea of going through the Panama Canal and everyone becoming fluent in Spanish. Until, that is, I discovered that once on the Pacific side of the canal, it can be up to fourteen days at sea before arriving in the Galapagos. And then, it can be twenty to thirty *more* days before arriving at the French Polynesian islands in the middle of the Pacific. Alrighty then. Our crew is definitely not up to that.

So, the question for us seemed to be: one year or two? Ally was just beginning the third grade when we started talking about a trip, which would mean taking her out of the public elementary school she attended and homeschooling—or rather, "boatschooling"—her while we traveled. My initial thought was if we were going to pull her out of school, we should go for the two-year trip and take advantage of the myriad of different countries we would be able to explore in the Eastern Caribbean. Although my opinion changed drastically the more I learned, I naively thought the Bahamas didn't offer enough in the way of culture, history, or foreign country experience.

"After all, they speak the same language, the Bahamian dollar is one-to-one with ours, so no exchange rate calculations, and no water means no wars," I pleaded the case for a two-year trip to Michael. As if he really needed convincing.

We started to refine the idea of a two-year trip, although one year was still a viable option. Michael insisted we agree to consciously check in before we committed to the second year, "I'm not willing to ruin our marriage to stay out."

Good point. It was important to remember that Michael left Massachusetts for his second trip with a fiancé and a dog. He came home with the dog. The ex-fiancé flew home from the Bahamas alone. She and Michael just could not live

8

together on the boat. We affectionately refer to this time as "The Chelsea Years." Chelsea was the dog.

Yep, we would evaluate in the Bahamas, after we had been out cruising for about six months, to determine if we wanted to continue heading south to the Caribbean, committing to eighteen more months, or turn around and return home.

Michael and I have complementary skill sets. We have never divided household tasks along "pink and blue" lines but rather by what we enjoy or do particularly well. For us, this means Michael generally tackles the budgeting from a high level, and I pay the bills and manage the details and taxes. We discuss major purchases, such as cars and rental properties, and we make plans together for things such as retirement, college, and vacations. This arrangement works well for us.

Michael took a pass at what a budget might look like for a two-year trip. It included the purchase of a catamaran, not nearly the size of *Field Trip*, but something stable where I wouldn't become seasick routinely. We talked through his budget—adding, taking away, or changing when necessary—for a couple of weeks. When Mark and Sarah came back through Massachusetts, we bounced our budget off of them.

"Does it sound reasonable?" Michael and I anxiously asked.

"Yes, mostly. Just increase the boat maintenance line. Then double it again," quipped Mark, quite seriously.

We sat on it. We talked it through some more. And it started to feel good.

I come from a family of pilots. My most treasured gift was the Rand McNally Atlas my dad gave me for Christmas my senior year of college. I studied abroad; I camped my way through the national parks. For work, as a technical consultant, I traveled every week, using the miles and points I accumulated to travel again for pleasure.

Michael was hooked at eighteen, when he *drove* from England to India. He, too, was a technical consultant, traveling every week, so it came as no surprise that when we married in 2003, our pace did not slow. Shortly after we got married, we spent six weeks on our boat, *Wayward,* sailing from Massachusetts to Nova Scotia and back, nearly 1,000 nautical miles.

It also came as no surprise that we bred a traveler, our daughter Ally. She first flew at six months; when she was three, we camped our way through the national parks in our RV for five months and again the following year for two months. We travel.

"Why are you doing this?" was a question we heard a surprising number of times.

For us, the answer is obvious: because we can. A big boat trip, like the two-week RV trip through Alaska when we got engaged and the six-week cruise to Nova Scotia right after we were married, and both of the RV trips while Ally was in preschool, was among a long list of adventures we have talked about since we met. Others include a bareboat charter in the Greek islands, a motorboat trip to the Great Lakes, and something big (a kayak and camping tour, a longer RV trip or charter or something) in Alaska, to name a few. And

New Zealand, Costa Rica, Ireland, Australia, Japan, South America, Croatia (a new addition), and Vancouver—there are so many places and ways to explore that one lifetime is just not long enough to do it all. To us, it seemed logical to take advantage whenever the opportunity arose. In order to do that, however, it was crucial that we had already talked about what was important to us (definitely not the high rolling lifestyle) and traveled down the road in terms of general plans.

This trip, along with others, may have come as a surprise to many, and it may even have appeared to be a rash decision to some. I assure you, it was neither. Will we go on every one of those grand adventures we have talked about? Unfortunately, I doubt it. Though when all is said and done, I imagine we will have taken far more trips than we would, had we never talked them through as dreamy ideas first, no matter how crazy they may have seemed.

Michael often says, "You may be able to travel again later, but you can never travel again now."

It's a mantra by which he, and now we, live. Take the trip. You will never regret it. Think you can't? You may very well surprise yourself. I sure did.

For the record, I am a gardener, not a sailor. Yet my inner traveler and adventure-seeker not only agreed to, but actually championed, our plan to spend two years living aboard a sailboat. Yep, let's pack up everything, rent our house, and move onto a 300-square-foot sailboat for two years. And in August of 2014, on Michael's fifty-fifth birthday, our crew of three—Michael, ten-year-old Ally, and I—did just that!

After "why," the next frequent question was, "I'd love to take two years off. How can you do it?" Generally, this was more of a rhetorical question, laced with equal parts envy and admiration. For those genuinely seeking an answer, I have written this book for you. In it, you will discover how we did it. Not *the* way, just one way. Our way.

This is the story about our decision to go, the two years of planning to make it work, and the first few months we lived aboard until we left the United States. To say I was pushed beyond my comfort zone in just about every direction is a vast understatement. Plus, at the age of forty-six, I had never before taught, let alone homeschooled. If you think the instruction manual for raising children is lacking, try homeschooling. And just contemplate the idea of puberty and menopause on a thirty-four-foot boat.

I still don't consider myself a sailor, even though we sailed *Ally Cat* for two years, from Massachusetts to Grenada and back—somewhere in the neighborhood of seven thousand nautical miles. I am giddy to be back in my gardens again; however, for anyone—sailor, gardener, and dreamer alike— seeking to live an intentional, authentic, and even unconventional life, a bit off of the beaten path, there may be some wisdom in our adventures. Perhaps some inspiration, too.

CHAPTER 2

CREW OF THREE

"Travel is fatal to prejudice, bigotry, and narrow-mind-edness, and many of our people need it sorely on these accounts. Broad, wholesome, charitable views of men and things cannot be acquired by vegetating in one little corner of the earth all one's lifetime." —Mark Twain

W e are a 9/11 story, Michael and I.

We were both consultants, implementing human resources and benefits systems for big companies. My client was the University of Pittsburgh, where I traveled four days a week. Michael joined the project part-time, working onsite every other week while he managed a number of other clients across the country on the off weeks. We were tippy-toeing around dating, each finding the other interesting, yet geographically undesirable. He lived in Massachusetts, and I lived in Nashville, Tennessee, having just moved there, and into my "perfect little stone cottage" from Virginia on September 1, 2001.

Finally willing to test the waters of dating, we made plans to meet in San Diego on September 13. We arranged to charter a sailboat for a few days after he met with a client in Los Angeles and attended a conference in San Diego. He was at home in Lexington, Massachusetts, and I was in Pittsburgh when we talked the morning of September 10. One of his other clients in Boston called with some sort of issue.

"I hope I can handle whatever it is by phone. If I have to go into the city, I'll never make my flight this afternoon, and I'll have to go out in the morning."

This meant he would fly from Boston's Logan International Airport to Los Angeles on Tuesday, September 11.

In shock, we watched the horrors as they unfolded in New York City that Tuesday morning. Then United Airlines Flight 93 went down after those fated words, "Let's roll," in a field in Somerset County, Pennsylvania, just a little more than 200 miles from where we sat on the thirty-fourth floor of the Cathedral of Learning at the University of Pittsburgh. Unsure of the extent of what was happening in our world, the university evacuated us immediately.

I imagine most of our coworkers went home to embrace their families. I certainly would have if I could. Instead, my fellow consultant and I went to my sterile corporate apartment. We had no idea what to do next; we were utterly lost. There was no cell service, as all circuits were completely overwhelmed. And we had no internet access as soon as we were evacuated. (This was long before smartphones and ubiquitous internet.) All we had was CNN on the television and my conversation with Michael from the day before playing over and over in my head.

"Do you think he made it to California?" I fretted.

Was Michael on the last flight from Boston to Los Angeles that made it before our world turned upside down? Or was he on United Flight 175, which we had just watched crash into the South Tower of the World Trade Center?

It was not until late that afternoon that I talked to one of Michael's coworkers, who let us know he was safe and sound in California. Thank God!

The world changed that day for many of us. The very same devastating events that affected so many lives in tragic ways positively changed Michael's and my life forever. It wasn't long until I realized that I cared for this man as much more than just a fun coworker. Having had his life spared, he, too, realized that he was ready to see where our tippy-toeing might lead.

Talk about life-changing. Two months later, we co-hosted Thanksgiving in his new house for his entire family. And six months after that, we were engaged. By the one-year anniversary of 9/11, I had sold my "perfect little stone cottage" in Nashville and moved to Massachusetts to marry Michael.

After the wedding in April 2003, we took a traditional honeymoon in Aruba for a week, enjoying a relaxed week of sun and fun and romantic dinners. Meanwhile, we were busy making plans for a six-week cruise in our sailboat, *Wayward,* north through Nova Scotia. Michael sailed to the Florida Keys one winter and to the Bahamas for another, and we took our boat out for a number of weekends and even a week-long vacation; this, however, would be *my* first attempt at *cruising.*

We easily settled in aboard *Wayward* and sailed from Buzzards Bay to Maine and across the Bay of Fundy to Yarmouth, Nova Scotia, whenever the fog allowed. Once we were around Cape Sable, amazingly, we had very little fog and perfect weather to thoroughly enjoy the delightful coastal towns of eastern Nova Scotia, including Shelburne, Liverpool, and Lunenburg. Unfortunately, by the time we arrived in Halifax, our furthest destination, I had been sick for more than ten days. I was more than ready to go see a doctor for some antibiotics for what we thought was bronchitis. Michael and I were both in for quite a surprise when we discovered it was not an upper respiratory infection. It was a baby!

Never one to take the easy way out, my pregnancy was difficult from the beginning and ended in an emergency C-section. So much for the detailed "birth plan" I wrote. Ever the planner, I had detailed out on paper every step of our baby's birth. "I plan, God laughs," as the sign hanging in our kitchen reminds me daily. Or, as Dwight D. Eisenhower famously said, "I have always found that plans are useless, but planning is indispensable."

In May 2004, however, our Canadian souvenir, Allison Lorrayne, was born. Our only goal was to leave the hospital with a healthy baby and a healthy mama, which we accomplished. After Michael and I barely survived five months of colic, Ally finally stopped crying and slept. Once she was no longer relentlessly crying and started sleeping like the proverbial baby, we discovered we actually enjoyed parenthood—which was a very good thing, as we had both grown up with multiple siblings in big, chaotic families and were planning the same in our home.

Ally was christened on a crystal-clear October day when she was six months old. I finally felt as if I had my "mommy legs" when they were unexpectedly kicked out from under me. My parents and both of my sisters were in Massachusetts for Ally's christening at our local church, which we joined when Ally was eleven days old. After our guests left, Mom and Dad had news to share: Dad had stage IV renal cancer. His doctors had not recommended any treatment, as there was no protocol for this advanced stage. He likely had only six to nine months to live.

I will forever be grateful for Michael's response to this devastating news when we discussed it that evening, "Go early and go often."

We drove to Virginia in November, as well as in December for Christmas. When we made the fourteen-hour trip yet again in January, Michael suggested Ally and I stay at Mom and Dad's.

"I can fly in and out of Roanoke, just as easily as Providence."

Michael has a sixth sense for knowing the right place to be.

With the able help of hospice, Mom and I were able to care for Dad at home, as was his wish, rather than in a hospital, for his final days. Though those were some of the most brutal weeks I have ever endured, I have no regrets. And the joy a baby can bring, even in the most trying times, is astonishing. What a paradox to hear gales of laughter as Mom fed Ally lunch while my sisters and I dressed Dad before the hearse arrived to transport him to the funeral home the day he died.

Ally and I moved back home to Massachusetts two weeks after the funeral. We all needed time and space to grieve and create a "new normal" without Dad. We arranged to return to Virginia within the month to celebrate Ally's first birthday.

And, it turned out, to deliver some wonderful news: we were expecting another baby. We were witnesses to the circle of life, the universe taking life and giving it back.

Unlike with Ally, this pregnancy started out smoothly. However, by the fourteenth week, I was on bed rest—not an easy task with an eighteen-month-old and a husband who traveled for work. I am not sure how we would have managed without the support—and meals and babysitting—from our church. After seven long weeks in bed, we were dealt a cruel blow. All of my amniotic fluid leaked out; twenty-two weeks was much too early for a viable baby. Three days later, just shy of twenty-three weeks, I delivered a stillborn baby. Our circle of life had been broken.

Somehow, we stumbled through the holidays, having piled unimaginable pain on top of our existing grief. I am eternally grateful for Ally, with her halo of blond curls and unreserved fascination with the world. Caring for her and sharing in her delight was the reason we got out of bed every morning. Time, that amazing healer of all things, saw us slowly emerge from the blanket of grief as dawn emerged from the darkness each morning.

Proving spirits are amazingly resilient, we decided again to try to expand our family. That winter, shortly after learning we were expecting again, we made an appointment with our doctor, given my pregnancy history, to discuss a strategy for our high-risk pregnancy. At ten weeks, full of hope, rather than a due date and a plan, we discovered there was no heartbeat. Crushed, we made the decision not to make any decisions for several months. As winter waned, though it was never our plan to have an only child, we decided we were not going to try again. Nor were we going to explore alternatives such as surrogacy or adoption, though we discussed it all.

Contrary to desire at times, life goes on. And it did for us, as well. God gave us one beautiful, healthy child, and we would spend our energies on her. Ally continued to learn and grow and enchant us. Though I went through the motions, I still was not at peace. I thought there should be more. And so I struggled to accept why we, a family with so much love to give, could not have more children.

Meanwhile, Mom made the decision to move to Colorado to be close to my oldest sister, Stacie. She was taking healthy steps to create her new normal. Was I ready to do the same? And then it happened. One day, as we were flying home from visiting Mom's new home, I looked across our row of seats, which the three of us filled perfectly, and thought, "This *is* my family." And in that one moment, the heartbreak and loss seemed to fade, and I experienced an immense sensation of peace, gratitude, and fulfillment.

Families come in all shapes and sizes, and my family is a family of three. It may not be big, but it's mine. That realization was a moment so poignant that it seems as if my life can be divided into "before" and "after." Once I accepted our family of three—my Crew of Three—I was no longer waiting. I wasn't waiting for the rest of my family or for anything else to arrive. I was ready to live, to truly completely live.

So, what can we do with only one child that we might not do with a flock? With our passion for adventure and exploration, it seemed only natural that travel would be a big part of it.

I was introduced to the joys of traveling as a child and continued to explore my world any chance I could through my twenties and thirties. Michael did not travel much as a child; however, he caught the travel bug the year after graduating from high school, when he had the incomparable opportunity to drive from England to India. Once we joined forces, we did not slow down. Apparently, our six-week sail to Nova Scotia was just the beginning!

I was at home with Ally, chasing an active toddler around, managing our new rental properties, keeping the books for Michael's consulting company, and gardening. Michael was still a technical consultant, traveling four days a week, implementing benefit systems, though he had gone out on his own as an independent consultant. The beauty of this arrangement was that we had flexibility with our time *and* the money to travel. So often, you have one without the other. We decided to introduce Ally to the United States and camp our way through the national parks in an RV. I took a similar trip in my twenties after being laid off from a job. Then, we were two girls with a tent in my little Honda Accord; our Crew of Three RV trip was going to be a little different.

As Ally started preschool, we set out to buy an RV for our adventure. What type and size? At the time, we were not "truck" people, so we ruled out trailers and fifth wheels. We really liked the A-class bus-type vehicles, as the enormous front windows allow great visibility to take in all the scenic views, but the floor plans seemed more suited for a couple—perhaps retirees?—than a family. We settled on a C-class, which is a smaller version of the bus-style A-class RVs, with a comfortable sleeping area in the back for us and the perfect space for Ally to sleep above the driver's seats. This area, which became known as "Ally's Attic," would easily accommodate piles of books, all of Ally's "friends" (that is, her stuffed animals), and of course, a three-year-old. Thirty feet seemed a good length, as we did not want anything too big once we added our towed vehicle.

Once we determined the type and size of RV we wanted and created our list of other criteria (age, mileage, etc.), finding our rolling condo was pretty easy. Michael found one that met our needs—and wants—in New Jersey, not far from where he was working at the time. After looking at it and taking it for a drive, he was ready to make an offer. He took pictures and described each in detail to me. Without either Ally or me seeing it, and with my encouragement, he made an offer, bought her, and drove her home to Massachusetts.

Did I say "her?" We bought a twenty-nine-foot Winnebago Minnie, which had a big "W" on each side. As soon as Ally saw it, utilizing her new-found preschool ABCs prowess, she said, "W, W, W is for William." He, the RV that is, was officially named *William*, immortalizing one of her preschool classmates. Though vessels are almost always referred to as "she" or "her," a centuries-old English-language tradition, *William* was definitely a "he" or "him."

Next came the fun part for me: outfitting the RV and planning our trip. Based on Michael's project schedule, we set the first weekend in February 2008 as our departure day. But his project did not end; in fact, it was extended for another year. We, however, were all geared up to go, so Michael quit, and we hit the road.

While we were most excited about visiting the national parks out west, when leaving Massachusetts in February, the only reasonable direction to head is south. Our primary goal was to find sunshine and warm weather. Our first stop was in Maryland—where we stayed the night with Julie, my partner in crime from my first cross-country camping trip.

Julie and her husband have three girls just a little older than Ally. After dinner, the four girls disappeared upstairs for a slumber party while the four adults enjoyed conversation and wine around a fire in the den. Julie and I couldn't help comparing the two cross-country camping trips. Dubbed the "Lemonade Tour 1994" (I had just been laid off from my job, and I was trying to make the best of my unexpected time of), we set off in my little Honda Accord for six weeks to explore the national parks of the West with a two-person tent, a cooler, and *very* little money. In contrast, Michael, Ally, and I were embarking on a life of relative luxury in *William*, including running water, a bathroom and a shower, a full kitchen complete with a coffee maker, a refrigerator *and* freezer, and real beds.

After spending time with friends in Virginia and South Carolina, it was time to actually spend our first night in *William* in St. Augustine, Florida. Perhaps we should have taken *William* on a test trip—or at least spent one night in him at home in the driveway—before setting off to live in him for five months. Luckily we adapted to our new life in *William* quite easily.

We planned a two-week vacation in Naples, Florida, to unwind and figure out how to live in our new home. We also visited our first national park of the trip, the Everglades.

Relaxed and thawed out, we headed west—Orlando to New Orleans to Dallas, and finally into New Mexico. We covered a lot of miles in a hurry to get to Carlsbad Caverns, our first national park of the West. Sadly, our timing was off to experience the thousands of Brazilian free-tailed bats that rush out of the natural entrance every evening at dusk to feed from April through October. While exploring some of the more than one-hundred underground caves amid stalactites and stalagmites, we learned about cave pearls, popcorn, and many other features adorning the limestone caverns.

Packing for our RV adventure was tricky. We left Massachusetts in the middle of the winter, spent time at the beach in Florida, skied in Colorado, and camped in California in both the heat at the beach as well as in the much colder Sierra Nevada Mountains. We sweltered in Utah and Arizona and camped in the snow in Wyoming and Montana. By far the biggest temperature swing we experienced in a single day was from 28 degrees Fahrenheit at Mono Basin National Forest, outside of Yosemite National Park, in the eastern Sierra Nevada Mountains of California, to 104 degrees Fahrenheit in Death Valley National Park, located partially in California and partially in Nevada. The aptly named Furnace Creek camping area was brutally hot, and yet, Death Valley boasted some of the most dazzling colorful rock formations we saw anywhere, particularly along Artists Drive.

Michael and I often traded "Ally Days" so that each of us could enjoy some of the more difficult hikes on our own. There were plenty of easy-to-moderate hikes that were suitable for all of us; however, there were abundant incredible hikes that were either too long or too technical for Ally. On my previous cross-country trip, I hiked to the bottom of the Grand Canyon, camped overnight at Bright Angel Campground, and hiked out the next day. Michael, on the other hand, had never even *seen* the Grand Canyon. Just as it was during my first cross-country trip, the Grand Canyon was again one of the highlights of our RV trip, as well.

We started on the North Rim, where we camped right on the rim of the Grand Canyon in the National Forest. Michael set out from the North Rim and hiked to the bottom, where he stayed the night at Phantom Ranch Lodge (Did you know there is a bunk house with a pub at the bottom of the Grand Canyon?) before hiking out to the South Rim. Ally and I drove *William* all the way from the North Rim around to the South Rim, about 200 miles through the Indian reservations, to meet him. My reward the next day was a solo nine-mile hike to Indian Garden, about three-quarters of the way down the Bright Angel trail into the Grand Canyon. That spot, where I enjoyed my lunch in complete solitude overlooking the Colorado River, is a place I often visualize while I am meditating.

If you've never had the opportunity to drive or take a train across the United States, consider making it a priority. The diversity within our country is simply stunning. Though five months may seem like a long time, it was not nearly enough time to see it all! There were so many places where we wanted to stay longer.

We are often asked about our favorite place. Narrowing it down to one is next to impossible; however, southern Utah emerged as our favorite area. With five spectacular national parks to explore—Zion, Bryce Canyon, Canyonlands, Arches, and Capitol Reef, collectively known as the Mighty Five—plus the charming town of Moab, we easily could have spent five months in Utah alone. Of course, then we may never have experienced Glacier or Yellowstone, Antelope Canyon or Joshua Tree, Badlands or Mount Rushmore, Grand Teton or Yosemite—so many places to explore and trails to hike.

By the numbers, we covered more than 12,000 miles in *William*, plus nearly 4,000 more miles in the car we towed, during our "Crew of Three - No Work - No School - Ward Family RV Adventure 2008." We explored seventeen National Parks and thirty-two states and took more photos than we will ever know what to do with—all while cementing our desire to live intentionally, which unquestionably would include adventurous travel.

Remember the job Michael quit to take this trip? They hired him right back as soon as we returned home. However, in February 2009, it really did end.

While we were in New Orleans in 2008, we were shocked to discover that many neighborhoods destroyed by Hurricane Katrina in 2005 had still not been rebuilt. The idea of taking *William* back to Louisiana to help with the rebuild kept swirling through my head. When I broached the subject with Michael, his response was, "New Orleans is far."

That year, as we hosted Thanksgiving, we had a slide show of photos from our cross-country trip playing on the television in our living room for family members to enjoy. Late in the evening, both happy and exhausted, Michael and I shared a hug and a quiet moment as we watched some of the memories of those five precious months scroll by. He looked at me and asked, "How would you feel about going back to Utah this winter when my project ends?" And he thought New Orleans was far!

A year after our first cross-country trip in *William,* we set out again, this time for two months. We limited the scope of the second trip to Florida, Utah, and Colorado, again pulling Ally out of her second year of preschool.

It appeared we had the hang of the Crew of Three traveling thing. Where to next? One if by land, two if by sea.

CHAPTER 3

SON OF A SAILOR

"We are all apprentices in a craft where no one ever becomes a master." —Ernest Hemingway

M ichael has sailed his entire life. He can't remember a time he didn't sail. When he and his older sister, Beth, and two younger brothers, were kids and lived in Upstate New York, his dad had a tiny eleven-foot Sailfish sailboat. Toting that little boat around on the top of the family car, he taught them all how to sail.

Later, when his dad bought a twelve-foot sailboat with a draft (the part of the boat under the water) that needed a trailer, it was a really big deal! With the Sailfish on top of the family car and the twelve-footer towed behind, they sailed the lakes and reservoirs nearby, often meeting family and friends for a day on the water. The only requirement for a road trip was a boat launch at the destination. Even before the internet, their dad found special places to sail, like Great Sacandaga Lake in the foothills of the Adirondack Mountains. Beth, four years older than Michael, also remembers summer vacations in Long Beach Island, New Jersey, where she and her dad would rent little Sunfish boats, the bigger cousin of the Sailfish, even before he bought their little boat.

Michael was twelve when his family moved from New York to Lexington, Massachusetts. By that time, he was a competent enough sailor to take the family boats out on his own, though the logistics of getting the boats to and in the water was problematic. He and his eleven-year-old brother, John, quickly discovered Community Boating in Boston. They spent many summer days sailing on the Charles River, enjoying both the classes that were available and, more importantly, the opportunities to borrow sailboats.

Together, Michael and John would walk to Lexington Center and hop on a bus to Arlington Heights, where they would catch another bus into Harvard Square. From there, they would take the Red Line to Charles Street, walk across the footbridge over Storrow Drive, and down to the river. The bus from Lexington to Arlington Heights didn't run frequently; however, it was an easy four-mile bike ride from Lexington. Or a long walk after Michael's bike was stolen one summer. Sometimes they scored a ride. But they managed to get there, and a day of sailing on the Charles River was worth whatever it took.

When Michael was in college, his dad bought a twenty-foot Barnegat sailboat. *Silver Fox*, as she was called, was kept at the South Boston Yacht Club. Since Michael went to college at nearby Northeastern University, he and his dad still regularly enjoyed sailing together. It was during this time that Michael started to read and take courses to really learn about tides and currents. And how to stay out of the way of big ships.

I suppose it should come as no surprise that Michael's very last class to graduate was a sailing class, which he took in the fall of 1983. After working alternating semesters in Northeaster's payroll office as a co-op throughout college, he took a job in the payroll department with Store 24 after the holidays. His plan was to walk in Northeastern's vast graduation ceremonies at the Boston Garden on Father's Day weekend in 1984. In April of that year, he and his dad took a ski trip to Breckenridge, Colorado, where his dad, age fifty-two, died from a heart attack. Needless to say, the graduation ceremony was the furthest thing from his mind just two short months later on Father's Day.

Meanwhile, Michael's sister, Beth, completed graduate school at Boston University, where she, too, had taken advantage of the sailing opportunities with Community Boating on the Charles. Enjoying sailing more and more, she and Michael made a plan to wander around the New England Boat Show together in February 1986. Dreaming of warmer days on the water, they climbed aboard some of the new Catalina 22s displayed at the show. As you might see at a car dealership lot, each boat displayed a pricing sign bragging about its low monthly payment.

Looking at each other, they said, "Hey, we can afford that!"

They could, and they did. After doing some research, much to their delight, they discovered for the same amount of money, they could afford an even bigger used boat. Together, in the spring of 1986, Michael and Beth bought *Mad Hatter*, a twenty-six-foot Pearson sailboat, for $14,000, financing most of the cost. By the summer, they were sailing her out of Fairhaven, Massachusetts, not far from where Beth went to college and now lived again.

Michael, who lived in Boston about an hour away, spent almost every weekend on *Mad Hatter* from April through October, either sailing or working on her. He took *Mad Hatter* south one very cold winter, making it as far as the Florida Keys. Unfortunately, the weather never cooperated that year for him to cross the Gulf Stream over to the Bahamas; however, the Florida Keys were a much better (and warmer) place to spend the winter than New England.

He continued to expand his sailing knowledge, taking United States Coast Guard Auxiliary and United States Power Squadron courses. He also honed skills in boat and engine maintenance, reading many books and magazines and applying what he learned on *Mad Hatter*. The author Malcolm Gladwell shared his "10,000 Hour Rule of Mastery" in his 2008 book *Outliers: The Story of Success*. This is the idea of expanding your abilities day after day, year in and year out, and is precisely what Michael did with sailing and sailboats all through his twenties and thirties.

Ten years later, when he was planning another trip south, he and Beth sold *Mad Hatter* for $5,000. (Whatever your reasons are for buying a boat, "as an investment" should not be among them.) Splitting the proceeds, Beth opted to keep her half in savings for a time in the future when she might sail more. She had two young children, worked full time, and her husband was not a fan of sailing. (In 1988, when she got married, her husband made it clear that he married her and not the boat.)

Michael was looking for a bigger, more seaworthy boat to take to the Bahamas. He determined that, as with his cars, he would not pay for his next boat by financing it with a loan again. Unlike a mortgage for a house, which *is* an investment and can create deductions at tax time, Michael could see there was really no upside to financing a boat. So he saved and bought *Wayward*, a 1973 Tartan thirty-four-foot sailboat, for $28,000.

Wayward is the boat I married, or at least married into. Although I was not a sailor, I understood that when we got married, I was marrying the man, the boat, and the lifestyle. I actually fell in love with Michael, or at least realized that I was in love, while sailing with him on *Wayward* in Buzzards Bay. He had such an easy grace aboard that he made it seem so natural. I realized, watching him single-hand her, that there was so much more to this man than what I saw at work as a technical consultant. This other side of him—the sailor— is who he really is.

Remember, I am a gardener, not a sailor. I also kayak and hike and bike and run and travel and write. I grew up swimming competitively and spending summer vacations at the beach. I was a lifeguard for years and have always loved the serenity of the water, be it an ocean, a lake, or a river. Even a creek will do. Both in high school and in college, I had friends with power boats. In my teens, I spent a fair amount of time in powerboats on the Potomac River and then in college on Mountain Lake, but there was virtually no sailing while I was growing up. In my twenties, I occasionally had the opportunity to spend a day aboard a sailboat and once even crewed. Okay, so I was dead weight for a J/24 sailing race in Annapolis. I enjoy being in the water or on the water in any kind of boat. I just never had the opportunity to learn how to sail.

Once we were married, Michael thought (hoped?) I would become more interested in sailing. He often said that I would enjoy it more the more I learned. It's not that I didn't enjoy it. I love sailing! Or rather, I love being on the sailboat. I just never felt the need to learn much about sailing it or maintaining it the first decade we were married. Michael was fully capable of single-handing *Wayward,* and it really felt like his boat. It *was* his boat. Especially after Ally was born and I became preoccupied with caring for her, I was more than content to have Michael handle the boat while I entertained the baby. Or napped with her.

As we started planning our trip and I was actively engaged in the purchasing process, I really did start to take much more of an interest in all things sailing. Once we bought our new boat in 2012, and my name was on the deed alongside Michael's, it was *our* boat in all ways. Michael gave me, for Christmas that year, a copy of Suzanne Giesemann's empowering book, *It's Your Boat Too: A Woman's Guide to Greater Enjoyment on the Water.*

With my newfound enthusiasm, I signed up for a twelve-week Advanced Coastal Navigation course given by the United States Coast Guard Auxiliary in Woods Hole, Massachusetts, about forty-five minutes away. The class was terrific, both in all I learned as well as for my confidence. It was a long winter driving nearly an hour to and from the Cape for a three-hour class every Wednesday night after work, but I learned a tremendous amount of useful information.

I had also hoped to take the Sailing Skills and Seamanship class through the Coast Guard Auxiliary, but it was not offered before we left. My navigation instructor suggested I buy the book and go through the materials on my own. Great idea. In fact, I planned to incorporate it into Ally's boatschooling curriculum, so we completed the course together. We took turns reading aloud to each other, took a pretest, discussed what we missed, then took the test for real. I certainly learned more (and had more fun) with that method than I would have had I simply read it on my own. I'm betting Ally did, too.

Although it certainly felt good to be armed with some book knowledge as we set out on our two-year sailing adventure, I lacked practical experience in an actual sailboat. Truth be told, I still do. Though I managed to get from Massachusetts to Grenada, I still don't think of myself as a sailor. It would be helpful for me to get out in a small boat. At least, that is what every good sailor I know has suggested.

Ally, like Michael, was raised on boats. When she was a baby and struggled with colic, practically the only time she slept was when she was in a sling attached to one of us or strapped into her car seat while moving. Michael affixed eye straps to tether her car seat to the boat, one set in the cockpit and another set in the salon below. She was as secure aboard *Wayward* as she was in the car. Needless to say, we spent a lot of time on *Wayward* the summer after Ally was born. Sometimes, we even left the mooring!

We live on the water, and Ally would clearly be spending a lot of time on boats, so it made sense to start her in swim lessons at the YMCA as soon as we could. She was definitely a water baby, easily swimming off the boat by the time she was three or four.

At six, when she was old enough to take sailing lessons at our town beach, we signed her up. The two-week, half-day program taught Ally basic sailing nomenclature and safety rules and consisted of both shore lessons and on-the-water instruction in Optimists, which are a type of small sailing dinghy specifically designed for children. She was enthusiastic and did well with the classroom knowledge, but was very timid and never felt quite comfortable going out alone in the Optis, as they are more commonly known.

After a second year at our town beach, Ally was old enough to go to the sailing camp at the YMCA. Ally loved this full-day, two-week camp because, in addition to sailing, the kids also enjoyed open swim sessions at the pool, where her cousin Becca was the pool director and a lifeguard. After gaining some confidence, Ally happily sailed the two-person 420s, one of the most popular training boats for kids.

Ally still resisted going out alone in a boat, and I never wanted to force it. The last thing I wanted was to create a fear—or at minimum, a dislike—of sailing. I sometimes question whether I could have encouraged her more effectively, though I never blamed her for her reluctance. To this day, though I have confidently kayaked *many* solo hours and taken the dinghy out by myself, I have still never sailed alone.

Once we were living aboard, Ally had a lot of fun sailing dinghies with other cruiser kids in the Virgin Islands and Grenada, and she even raced with her dad in local small boat regattas a couple of times since we got home. She was amazingly competent in the dinghy, which is akin to the family car when you live on a boat, zooming everywhere once we gave her the freedom to do so at the age of eleven.

The summer after we got home, Ally asked to go to a two-week sailing camp at Beverly Yacht Club in the next town, where the sailing was a bit more serious than at the YMCA. She really gained confidence at the helm and sailed solo in the 420s that year. She thought she might want to be a camp counselor at the YMCA, perhaps even a sailing instructor, so I guess we did not ruin sailing for her after all. Turns out, like her cousin, Ally took the lifeguard route for summer jobs, guarding at nearby Fort Phoenix State Reservation beach.

Like Michael, Ally has time and opportunity on her side if she chooses to master the art of sailing—if it is *her* passion. And if she decides to marry an Aussie and live on a sailboat somewhere in the French Polynesian islands, Michael and I will be reaping exactly what we have sown. Of course, she may have to come to the Bahamas if she wants to see us in the winter.

One final note, or word of caution, if you will. If you own boats, you probably already know this, though if you don't, I feel compelled to warn you: I am pretty sure our boats reproduce in the yard. At last count, in addition to the Gemini, there are thirteen boats in our yard. They are only in the yard because it's the middle of the winter. Usually, most of them are out on the marsh or on moorings in our cove and are used regularly. And in our defense, three of them are Beth's—two kayaks and *Molly*, an Osprey 16 Daysailer. (Remember her half of the proceeds from the sale of *Mad Hatter*? About fifteen years ago, she decided it was time to reinvest them in her own boat, *Molly*.)

I have two kayaks, a single sit-on-top that went on our trip and a double kayak we used a lot more when Ally was little. Though Michael does not count kayaks, I do, so that accounts for five. How about the other six? There is *Rocket*, our dinghy, the AB inflatable we took on our trip; and *Alice*, the Trinka sailing dinghy we towed behind *Wayward*, which also rows like a dream; and *Matilda*, the aluminum fishing boat Michael bought for his fiftieth birthday; and, of course, the work skiff, to deal with the messy job of maintaining moorings; and *Ty*, and old dinghy and perhaps the only one Michael would part with, if we could find her under the Concord grape vines. Not long after we got home, we were given a Hobie Wave, the less serious little sister of the more popular Hobie Cat 16. Ally actually jumped up and down when she found out it was ours. (She is now a teenager, so we don't get that kind of unbridled joy much anymore!) Ally named her *Wild Cat,* and she may just be the most expensive *free* boat ever. But boy, do Michael and Ally get a thrill out of zipping around in her all summer.

When your boats start having babies in your yard, don't say I didn't warn you. Though, honestly, they are all a bit like children to me. So I actually do have that big chaotic family I always dreamed about.

As I write this, Michael and I have added "oyster farmer" to our resumes. We own and run a small four-acre shellfish farm growing oysters in town. After two years of barefoot pirate living, as you might imagine, long hours as a technical consultant under fluorescent lights failed to bring Michael much pleasure when we got home. To shorten his consulting years and still fund our retirement and Ally's college education, we invested in his sanity, diving headlong into the world of aquaculture. Talk about being outside our comfort zone.

Of course, neither *Matilda* nor the work skiff was exactly what we needed for this venture. Yep, you guessed it: another boat. Actually, two. Michael brought home a nineteen-foot Carolina Skiff, now known as *Frosty.*

In the initial two years of running Mattapoisett Oysters, our primary focus was learning how to keep our oysters alive. We aimed to nurture these delicate creatures from their initial state—spat no larger than a flake of red pepper— to a minimum size of three inches. Those that thrived were sold to a distributor, destined for half-shell platters. Once we managed to do that, we started to look at our processes and develop some better practices. Enter *Seal,* the most recent addition to our family. She is a twenty-six-foot Sun Tracker Pontoon boat—you know, a "party boat." Except we ripped out all of the comfortable seats and drink holders and now use it as a work platform for our oyster-farming activities. Why *Seal?* This particular pontoon boat used to be the Provincetown Seal Tour boat. Seriously, I can't make this stuff up.

CHAPTER 4

OUR FLOATING CONDO

"A boat is like a magic world, like a little island." — *Renzo Piano*

Though we already owned *Wayward* outright, the thought of managing seasickness full-time for two years was completely out of the question for me. Catamarans sail very differently than monohulls, with their twin hulls providing more stability. This change in motion virtually eliminated seasickness for me. Hence, our decision to sell *Wayward* and buy a new-to-us catamaran.

For budgeting purposes, we had to come up with a reasonably solid number to buy and outfit a boat. In order to do that, we needed to know what was out there that might meet our needs, so Michael started to research the used catamaran market. His favorite sites were www.yachtworld.com and www.sailboatlistings.com.

There are many ways to find and buy a boat. Some folks buy a boat with a loan and make regular payments, similar to a mortgage payment. Typically, we have seen that many of these cruisers plan to sell the boat at the end of their trip. At the opposite end of the spectrum are the people who sell their home and all their belongings, buy their boat outright, and sail for as long as it makes sense or until the money runs out. Of course, there are also many cruisers who already own a boat and deem it perfect for their adventure.

Still others were in a similar situation to ours. We live on the water, have always had a sailboat, and will likely always have one in the future. Our plan was to sell *Wayward* and buy a catamaran suitable for the trip and then keep it for the foreseeable future. It had to meet our needs to cruise for two years and be within our trip budget. Additionally, it also needed to be a boat we could afford and wanted to sail for the next decade or so.

Originally, our budget for buying and fixing up a boat was $125,000. Over time, we ended up increasing this to $150,000, basically because our finances allowed it. It's important to note, though, that if our finances had dictated, we could have, and would have, done it for $100,000. The increase gave us a few more of the "nice to have" items from our list.

Of course, had we not been in a position to buy a catamaran, and we categorically wanted to go cruising, we certainly could have taken *Wayward*. And *a lot* of meds to manage nausea. Having money to travel is important. But it's even more important to be flexible with what is "enough" and go! Be creative and make it happen. As Lin and Larry Pardey, basically the First Couple of cruising, have repeatedly said, "Go simple. Go small. Go now."

The only given was that our new boat would be a catamaran. The good news was for a catamaran in our price range, there were really only three boats available: Gemini, Prout, and PDQ. The internet is an amazing resource, as it allowed us to check out each of these boats, explore specs and floor plans, and see what was for sale and where. We probably would have looked harder at both the Prout and the

PDQ, as they are quite similar to the Gemini; however, there were none available for sale anywhere on the East Coast. Actually, there was one PDQ in Florida, but that particular boat was out of our price range.

During this time, we started to add to and refine our list of requirements, both "must haves" and "nice to haves." Other than the stability of a catamaran, I really had only two major requirements: an indoor shower and an easily accessible table. For ten years aboard *Wayward*, our 1973 34-foot Tartan, we used a solar camp shower hung from the boom in the cockpit. I wanted to be able to shower without getting naked on deck. Not unreasonable. Aboard *Wayward*, the table was a big semicircle of teak stored under a salon cushion. It was so heavy and awkward that I was not able to lift it out and set it up myself. We planned to live on this boat for two years, and in addition to three meals a day every day, Ally and I would use our new table for homeschooling, too.

Michael's criteria were a bit more involved. He wanted to be able to single-hand the boat as he always had, so thirty-two to thirty-six feet seemed an ideal length. He was looking for a diesel engine with a fairly low number of hours. Low is a nebulous term; however, what he was looking for was under 500 hours. Alternatively, he would consider a boat that had a lot of hours and needed to be repowered if the price was right. He also did not want a boat loaded with ten-year-old equipment. Preferably the boat we bought would be fairly stripped down in terms of electronics, so we could purchase and install our own updated choices. Finally, he wanted a screecher—a big lightweight headsail that would help us sail more easily downwind and in light winds. And once we saw our first Gemini, we added a hammock seat to our "must have" list. The hammock seat is a sling seating area aft of the cockpit, basically over the water, supported by the davits, the stainless steel scaffolding used to lift and store the dinghy. We deemed it our "happy place" from the moment we tried it out.

As a family, we went to Revere, Massachusetts, to see our first Gemini in person. Once we went aboard and looked around, we were convinced it would easily meet our needs. The Gemini 105Mc is a 34-foot catamaran with two quarter berth cabins in the aft, or rear, of the boat, one in each hull, and a master berth forward of the salon and galley, not to mention a very civilized front door leading into the salon. It has one head, with a cleverly designed shower. And I *loved* the wide-open salon with its vast built-in table! One of my first thoughts was, "I can definitely see homeschooling Ally here." It was the perfect size and layout for our Crew of Three.

It quickly became a one-boat search: the Gemini 105Mc. There were a number available on the East Coast—some in the Boston area, not far from where we live, some in Florida, not far from where Michael worked, and quite a few in Annapolis, where they were made. As luck would have it, when Michael traveled to Florida every other week for work, he had to stop and change planes at Baltimore Washington International (BWI) airport in Maryland. We used this to our advantage for him to scout out a fair number of boats in Annapolis.

Michael stayed an extra day in Florida to check out several Geminis within driving distance of Jacksonville. He didn't see anything that warranted a second look. That, coupled with the more complicated logistics of getting a boat from Florida back to Massachusetts, led us to focus our efforts on the Annapolis area. So Michael stopped in Maryland on his way home to see what was available there.

Headquartered in Ft. Lauderdale, Florida, The Catamaran Company opened the Annapolis Catamaran Center in 2005. The company purchased a majority interest in Performance Cruising Inc., the manufacturer of Gemini Catamarans, in 2009. Annapolis Catamaran Center moved into the Gemini Headquarters and was renamed The Catamaran Company-Annapolis. Gemini Catamarans and The Catamaran Company-Annapolis are still located in the old waterfront manufacturing facility in Annapolis.

We contacted the Catamaran Company-Annapolis and enlisted the services of a broker. In mid-November, Michael stopped in Annapolis once again, and I flew down to meet him. We had a busy day, as our broker arranged for us to see five boats. By the end of the day, *Double Pinocle* emerged as the frontrunner. She was a 2004 Gemini 105Mc. Her Westerbeke diesel engine had only 410 hours, and other than a trio of standard Raymarine electronics (wind, depth, and speed), the only other electronics onboard were a small Garmin GPS and a Raymarine autopilot. Though she was eight years old (the same vintage as Ally), the interior was in terrific shape. She had obviously been well-maintained by the sellers, who were the original owners. The galley and head looked barely used—in fact, we later discovered the plastic protective coating on the oven had never been removed.

Michael and I flew back to Massachusetts together to host our annual Thanksgiving dinner, full of excitement and almost ready to make an offer. Since this was a big family decision, we took Ally with us to Annapolis to see *Double Pinocle* the day after Thanksgiving. Yep, she was the one. Happy captain, happy first mate, and happy crew equaled a happy Crew of Three!

Ready to make an offer, we sat down with our broker and crafted one to present to the sellers, then headed back to Massachusetts. Within the week, our offer was accepted, and a survey—similar to a home inspection when buying a house—and sea trial were arranged. Michael and I met in Annapolis once again, so we could both be on hand for this important step in the boat-buying process, as well as our broker and our surveyor, Peter Hartoff. What a thrill it was for us to raise her sails for the first time on that unseasonably mild December day.

Thoroughly checking every inch of *Double Pinocle*, the surveyor found only a few minor issues. We took her to a nearby marina to have her hauled in order to check out the underside and then relaunched—referred to as a short haul. While waiting, we enjoyed a nice lunch of Maryland crab cakes as we got the scoop from the surveyor. The most serious issue was with the portside centerboard, which would not go all the way up. The engine had a rough start, as well. Satisfied with the plan to fix what needed fixing and to schedule a separate engine survey, we came to an agreement with the sellers. They were a lovely couple and were more than generous in sharing their working knowledge of *Double Pinocle*.

After the engine survey went smoothly, a closing date was set: December 21, 2012. Less than five months after we hatched our plan, Michael, Ally, and I gave each other a bouncing baby boat for Christmas!

Though my name was also on the deed, Michael went to Annapolis alone for the closing. He moved *our* boat to the boatyard to have the centerboard fixed. We arranged to have her hauled out and power washed, have her bottom painted, and the engine winterized. Before she was launched in the spring, we also hired the boatyard to tune the rigging and wash and wax our girl.

Why didn't I go to Annapolis for the closing? The same day Michael signed the papers to buy *our* boat, I applied for a job with New Bedford Public Schools. Yep, it was time to make the finances work.

CHAPTER 5

MAKING THE FINANCES WORK

"A goal is a dream with a deadline." —Napoleon Hill

Michael took two long sailing trips before we met. After we got married, we planned and went on two RV trips together and a six-week sailing trip. Two things we know for sure: Michael's good at budgeting and I am good at planning. And we are able to live in small spaces together.

The initial budget for a two-year trip included the following sections: Buying the Boat, Fixed Costs, Operating Expenses, and Reentry. For budgeting purposes, so as not to get bogged down in details, we use whole numbers. And always round up. This keeps us focused on the big picture without getting stuck in the weeds. We started to add details and fine-tune the numbers to come up with our "Magic Number."

While it is possible to make a living while cruising, that was not our plan. We were interested in more of an unpaid sabbatical. Much of the attraction for us was the idea of completely disconnecting from our "normal" life. Therefore, other than rental income, our plans did not include any money coming in for two years.

Buying the Boat

This section included the purchase price, taxes, travel expenses incurred to buy the boat, costs to refit the boat to get her ready for cruising, plus costs to haul and maintain her until the trip. This also included any equipment we needed to buy: dinghy, life jackets, kayak, paddleboard, snorkel gear, etc. (For a more detailed discussion, see Chapter 8: Boat Projects and Online Boyfriends)

Total: $150,000

Fixed Costs

This section included insurance—boat, health, life, and disability—as we were not willing to take the risk of dropping these coverages while traveling. This also included our mortgage and tax liability and was somewhat offset by income from our rental properties.

Total: $46,000

Operating Expenses

We budgeted $4,000 per month for spending for the two years, which included food, toiletries, entertainment, fuel, boat maintenance, everything. We added $6,000 for a single trip home halfway through and $5,000 per year for "unexpected boat issues or other emergencies."

Total: $112,000.

Reentry

When we finished our trip, we would need some cash to get settled back in—one car, and perhaps two, cellphones, a new winter wardrobe for Ally. Haircuts. Shoes.

Total: $38,000

Our Magic Number, or "Money to Go Far," as Michael called this spreadsheet: $346,000

If we chose to sell our home or either of our rental properties or were willing to dip into our retirement savings or Ally's education fund, we could have set sail almost immediately. Alternatively, we calculated we could patiently save for two years, thereby reserving those investments for their intended purposes. For us, the plan-and-save method was a no-brainer as it posed a much lower risk in the long term. Plus, we were not in a rush to go; in fact, the two years gave us time to get ready. And that decision looked even better in the rearview mirror, particularly as college and retirement loomed.

While Michael was scouting out boats, I set about accounting for what we had spent so far in 2012. Once I had detailed every dollar, we were easily able to identify where we spent our money. We discovered we spent a lot of money eating out and a significant amount on books and chiropractic care. I also spent a fair amount on clothes for Ally and me, yoga, and reflexology. If you have never gone through this type of exercise, give it a whirl. It provides invaluable information.

Armed with that knowledge, we started to save immediately. Every dollar we saved put us that much closer to our goal. We still ate out some, though we chose less expensive restaurants. We opted for pizza versus the upscale Italian restaurant, and sushi was reserved for special occasions. We started using the library more and Amazon less. I searched out free and inexpensive books to load onto our Kindles, both for school and pleasure. I cut down to one yoga class a week, and Michael and I both got serious about stretching and exercising daily. This kept our backs and hips healthy and happy and allowed us to cut back on the chiropractic visits, which led to more self-sufficiency. A positive outcome of my new job was I didn't have time or energy to shop beyond necessities. My biggest extravagance was the daily 99-cent iced coffee from the McDonald's drive-thru to give me enough of an energy boost to make it through homework, dinner, and bedtime.

We canceled our cleaning lady. Then quickly rehired her. Michael and I have always divided up household chores based on what we each were good at or what we liked to do. Unfortunately, neither of us liked to clean. Give me a garden to weed, a lawn to mow, or shrubs to prune, and I will choose it over mopping the kitchen floor any day—and twice on Sundays! Not surprisingly, the addition of a full-time job did not make cleaning the house any more appealing to me. To reach our goals, we needed to spend less and save more, yet my mental health was important, too.

Every month, Michael would go back to our budget, enter current numbers, and figure out how much more we needed to reach our Magic Number. We had almost all of our accounts—personal, business, and rental—with Bank of America. Their office is conveniently located for us, and I love their simple online banking. However, we have always kept one completely separate savings account at First Citizens. Something about "out of sight, out of mind" works for us. We used the First Citizens account to accumulate funds for our cruising kitty. It bordered on elation every time we made a deposit. It was tangible evidence we were getting closer to our dream one step at a time.

In addition to our cost-cutting measures, we took a good look at our current assets. Where else could we "find" money? We had regular savings, our emergency fund, some stocks, our retirement accounts, Ally's college fund, an RV, a boat, two rental properties, and our home. My ability to work outside the home was also an asset.

We verified how much money we had in regular savings, as well as in our emergency fund. When we married, we were both consultants, meaning one or both of our incomes could end abruptly. We aim to keep about twelve months' worth of expenses in an emergency fund at all times, an amount that makes us comfortable. Though we never seriously considered raiding either our retirement accounts or Ally's education fund, there was comfort in knowing the amount in all of those accounts, even if drawing from them would be a last resort upon our return. This meant that the $38,000 earmarked for reentry could be something of a soft amount.

Michael's dad worked for General Electric for years. When he died in the early 1980s, he left a significant amount of GE stock to Michael's mom. Over the years, she had gifted numerous shares to Michael, each of his three siblings, and all seven of her grandkids. Our plan was to hold on to it until it was time to pay for college. We calculated the shares we owned were worth about $10,000. We agreed to sell it, adding the proceeds to our growing kitty. Keeping this amount in mind, and depending on how our reentry finances looked, we hoped to be able to move this money into Ally's college education account when we returned, which we did.

As consultants, we were self-employed. This arrangement, while clearly involving some risks, also came with some significant benefits. We were able to contribute much more money into our retirement account, a simplified employee pension or SEP IRA, than employees are allowed in a 401(k) or 403(b) retirement savings plan. Traditional employee contributions in 2011 were capped at $16,500 per year; however, we were able to contribute as much as 25 percent of our net earnings per year, up to $49,000.

In 2011, with our earnings and expenses, we were able to put away close to $40,000. By diverting our planned retirement contributions for 2012 and 2013, we added $60,000 to the cruising kitty with little effort. I know, I know $40,000 plus $40,000 equals $80,000. The "missing" $20,000 went to taxes, the result of not making retirement contributions for two years. It is also important to note that this adventure clearly pushed back our retirement plans by at least four to five years: two years of diverted savings, two years not working or contributing, plus the year we returned, when we would unlikely be able to contribute again.

Considering our other assets, we planned to sell *William*, the RV, and *Wayward*, the sailboat. To do so would take some work, so we made the lists and started the process.

We bought *William*, a 2003 29-foot Winnebago Minnie, in 2007 for $40,000 for our five-month cross-country trip. Six years later, he had been a faithful companion for two cross-country trips, plus countless camping excursions to New Hampshire. We also discovered he was the ideal tailgate vehicle for Patriots games and the perfect mobile potty for beach days with kids.

By the summer of 2013, with our sailing adventure taking precedence, *William* had been neglected for much of a year. I suppose to keep him from getting lonely, a family of mice took up residence. Ewwww. Due to their damage, we had to rebuild several rather gross drawers, as well as tear out and replace the carpet. During a service station mishap in California, *William's* rear bumper was badly mangled. At the time, we hired a body shop to straighten it out, and then we bandaged him up with white electrical tape to keep the rust at bay. It worked for us, but to sell, the bumper definitely needed to be replaced.

Recreational Vehicles are an awful lot like boats in that they often leak from above, and *William* was no exception. We fixed some water damage, cleaned up a little rust, installed a new freshwater pump, and put him on the market.

It was a bittersweet morning in August 2013 as we watched *William* drive up Meadowbrook Lane for the last time. He went to a good home with an adventurous couple, which made it a little easier. We knew it was part of the plan, but we still would miss him. We have a treasure trove of memories, and it's a reasonable assumption our RV days are not over.

Add $25,000 to the kitty!

As we waved goodbye to *William,* we knew it was time to get *Wayward* in shape and sold. Michael made sure her diesel was running well, checked the bilge pumps, and cleaned the bilges. He rebuilt the head, replacing the seals, valves, O-rings, and other components located inside the head's hand pump, and refilled freshwater tanks. She needed a good cleaning and to have some missing teak trim bits replaced. Michael wanted to use *Wayward's* self-tailing winches and year-old batteries on our new boat, so he swapped them out.

The biggest task on *Wayward* was to fix a large portion of her decks, which were soft with water penetration. Michael cut out huge sections of her deck with a skill saw. He followed the soft wood, grinding out all the rotted areas, sometimes using a hammer and chisel, all while she was perched on boat stands in our yard, still covered from the winter with shrink wrap. He glued in foam and built the fiberglass back up. After fairing the fiberglass, to create a surface without bumps or hollows, he primed where he made the repairs.

At last, it was time to paint the decks, put the hardware back on, and get her sold.

Painting was a two-person sport. Michael put on the first coat; I followed behind, adding the glossy top coat and non-skid where it was needed. Standing back, checking out our handiwork the next day, I marveled, "We make a pretty good team!"

If you had told me twenty years ago that I would be painting newly restored decks on a boat with my husband and planning a two-year sailing trip with our family, I would have thought you were crazy. Certifiable, in fact.

Once everything was dry, the final step was to reattach the stanchions. These are the stainless-steel tubes attached to the deck with backing plates. Stanchions provide the scaffolding to hold lifelines, the plastic-coated stainless steel wire rope ostensibly keeping everyone on the boat rather than in the water.

I was topside, holding the first stanchion in place, drill in hand, ready to put the holes through our newly restored deck for the screws. I was timid at first, as I have little experience with power tools. "Tell me when," I said nervously.

Michael was down below, holding the backing plate, waiting for me to drill through.

"Okay, ready," from below. Then, "Push harder!"

I did, and the first hole was done. I boasted, "Hey, I've got this!"

"Go to the next hole."

"Ready?"

"Yep."

Feeling pretty confident, I pushed hard from the start.

"YOWSER!!" An expletive I have never heard from Michael before or since.

Uh oh. I dropped the drill and ran below, meeting Michael in the cockpit. Blood was everywhere, and he had a towel wrapped around his hand.

"Oh my God. What did I do?!"

I drilled a hole through his thumb. I *definitely* shouldn't be trusted with power tools. Thankfully, he got down the ladder from the boat and up the stairs into our house before he went into shock. Sitting on the couch, though, his face turned white.

"We need to get to the ER," I stated, leaving no room for debate.

Once at the hospital, we found out the drill did not actually go all the way through his thumb, and the nail bed was not damaged. Whew. The nurses cleaned him up, bandaged his thumb, and gave him a tetanus shot for good measure. On the bright side, I could check updating Michael's tetanus shot off my list.

Good grief. While Michael will readily admit that he was holding the backing plate in the wrong place when he gave me the okay, he got a lot of mileage out of that story! Still does.

A couple of weeks later when Michael's thumb was not quite so tender, we finished reattaching the stanchions, without any more drama. I gave *Wayward* a thorough cleaning, bow to stern, and she went on the market.

The sales process didn't take more than a couple of months and went relatively smoothly. We priced the boat well, and we had about half a dozen potential buyers look at her. Most were serious and ready to buy a boat, though a few were lookie-loos early in their process. We had a reasonable offer within about six weeks.

Michael was upfront with the buyer, "She's an old boat. She has old boat issues. She's priced right, and I am not interested in fixing anything your surveyor finds."

The buyer agreed. However, he prudently hired a surveyor so he would know just what he was getting. The survey came back indicating some rot in the rudder. After getting a $1,500 quote to fix it, the buyer asked, "Would you consider splitting the cost to repair it?"

Michael was more than agreeable. We had a deal.

Several weeks later, the new owner arrived with two of his adult kids, duffels and sleeping bags in hand, to sail to her new home in Maine.

"The two happiest days in a boat owner's life are the day they buy a boat and the day they sell it," as the old joke goes. We were definitely still in the giddy stage after buying our new-to-us Gemini. Remembering how gloomy I was watching *William* drive away, I was not sure I agreed with the second half. However, I had never sold a boat before. After putting in so much hard work—sweat, tears, and even Michael's blood—to get *Wayward* ready to sell, watching her sail away from Brandt Island Cove elicited feelings of relief more than sadness.

Add another $12,000 to our savings.

When I was pregnant with Ally, Michael and I started talking about her education fund. We set up a traditional 529 college savings plan into which we made regular contributions. Additionally, we both liked the idea of owning property—not huge commercial properties, just small residential houses that could provide a little positive cash flow over the years and have the potential for a decent gain when sold. Though we fully realized that the real estate market can be fickle and unpredictable, we started to learn about the local rental market.

In April 2007, on our fourth anniversary, we purchased a three-family house in the Onset section of Wareham, Massachusetts, about twenty minutes from our house. We thought we would hold onto the property as a rental for about fifteen years, selling it to cover the cost of sending Ally to college. On the other hand, if Ally's education fund or scholarships covered her college expenses, we would have this property to help fund our retirement, as the mortgage would be paid off, and rents would provide some monthly income. Or we could sell it and buy one heck of a retirement boat!

We inherited three sets of tenants and proceeded to make just about every rookie landlord mistake imaginable. We generally only made the same mistake once, but there were plenty to be made. In 2011, either gluttons for punishment, fools, or simply optimists with failing memories, we decided to expand our real estate holdings. Our second investment property, a charming single-family home, was located in Onset, as well.

In addition to the Onset rental properties, we had to make some decisions about our home, as well. We definitely did not want to sell it. Unfortunately, in addition to a mortgage payment, our taxes, insurance, and mandatory flood insurance cost almost $25,000 per year. We paid close to $12,000 each for taxes and insurance annually! Somehow, we needed to cover these exorbitant expenses.

Ever the logical one, Michael said, "The only real way to cover our costs is to rent it out."

I hesitated, "I'm not sure I am ready to have *strangers* live in my *home*."

Were we ready to rent out our home? That's a tough one; however, in the end, the answer for us was "Yes."

Our decision to keep the two Onset properties and add our primary residence to the rental list meant we had to figure out who would manage it all while we were gone. My girlfriend, Laurie, grew up around rental properties as her parents owned a number of units in Ohio. In fact, her summer job in college was flipping apartments between tenants. We trust her wholeheartedly, and we knew she and her husband, Rob, would take good care of our properties, so we gave them the first right of refusal. We offered them the job at the going rate of 10 percent of collected rents per month. It could, after all, be decent money for what generally is a part-time job.

Until it is not.

We talked about this risk. Laurie is an eighth-grade science teacher with little flexibility during the school year; Rob is a university professor; however, he was on sabbatical the first year we were gone. They were willing to take on the risk, both to help us and to add some extra funds to their retirement and education accounts.

We thought if there was going to be any rental property drama, it would certainly come from our multi-family. Nope. Not the first year, at any rate. Little did we know that the winter we left was going to be one of the snowiest and coldest winters on record in Massachusetts. Our house was the troublemaker. Our poor tenant had to deal with frozen pipes, which meant no heat and no water, *four* times. The last episode resulted in broken pipes and significant damage to a bathroom. Poor Rob and Laurie dealt with a steady stream of plumbers, HVAC technicians, and other contractors all winter.

By the time Laurie and the kids, came to spend the week with us on the boat in the Bahamas for February vacation, they were at their wits' end. The only reason Rob wasn't in the Bahamas with us was that he was back in Massachusetts dealing with frozen pipes at *their* house!

As Laurie filled us in on the gory details of a winter we are very glad we missed, we reiterated what we said from the beginning, "We are not willing to ruin our friendship over this business arrangement. If it's too much, just say the word. We can find someone else to manage the properties."

She really wanted to be able to do it, and I could tell she was hesitant to give up. Until she got an email, while she was with us in the Bahamas, from one of the tenants in the multi-family, giving notice that she was moving out.

Uncle.

We reached out to all the real estate agents we had collaborated with over the years, seeking recommendations for property managers, but our efforts were fruitless. At that point, we were in a fairly populated area of the Bahamas, where we were able to use a local cellphone as a hotspot for internet access. Not long after Laurie and the kids made their way back to Massachusetts, we were preparing for five to six months of uncertainty as we sailed through the Eastern Caribbean to Grenada, a journey likely accompanied by unreliable internet with virtually no phone connectivity.

Finally, Michael put calls into the real estate companies in Onset—cold calls, really. One of these calls, to Jack Conway Realtor, resulted in a transfer to Danielle. As a weekend job, she handled their summer rentals, not property management.

"I am extremely organized and detail-oriented. A number of my coworkers and clients have suggested I try my hand at property management." She was upfront, "I have never done this before, but I am willing to give it a try if you are."

She liked the idea since it was a finite commitment—just the eighteen months until we returned to Massachusetts.

Our options were pretty limited, so we decided to take a flier on her. We continued to talk and iron out details. The more we talked, the more we were convinced it could work.

Danielle met with Laurie as a quasi-interview, if you will, and Laurie agreed with our assessment. Laurie notified the tenants of the change and transitioned the information, along with a pile of keys, to Danielle. And we were back in business. Cruising business, that is—not property management!

Hiring Danielle was one of the best decisions we made. Not only did she fill the one apartment immediately, but she found solid tenants for each of the other apartments in the multi-family within the next year. She also managed the remaining repairs to the bathroom in our house and had a new water heater installed in the single-family, not to mention insurance and town inspections and a host of other responsibilities. After almost eighteen months, I think Danielle was thrilled to hand my files back over—and the pile of keys.

Rental adventures aside, between the three houses, we anticipated we would realize about $1,300 per month in net income. Add $31,000 to the bottom line.

Though higher retirement contributions are a definite plus to being self-employed, one drawback is the responsibility of providing all our own insurance—medical, life, and disability. In 2011, health insurance for our family of three cost approximately $1,500 per month.

"What can I do jobwise to get medical benefits?" I mused to Michael. I didn't really need a huge salary, given the fact we would automatically save $18,000 per year by eliminating our insurance premiums.

In 2012, when we started planning this adventure, Ally was in third grade, only eight years old, and still little. Having had the privilege of being home with her since she was born, I wanted to find a job that would allow me to be with her in the mornings as well as after school. A job in a school seemed ideal, and though I'm not qualified to teach, I certainly had the skills to work as a teacher's assistant, what is called a paraprofessional, or "para" for short, here in Massachusetts. I knew jobs would be few and far between in our desirable district; however, I felt certain I would easily be hired in New Bedford. Located less than five miles from us, New Bedford is one of the poorest performing—and poorest—school districts in the state. However, they offered health insurance to their paras!

I checked out the New Bedford Public Schools website, noting a number of openings. I downloaded an application and set about collecting the necessary information to complete my package. It had been a *very* long time since I needed employment recommendations, let alone college transcripts. And it was entirely fitting that I submitted my job application the same day Michael was in Annapolis closing on our new boat: December 21, 2012.

As soon as school was back in session after the holidays, I received a call about an opening. After talking for less than thirty minutes, the human resources gal asked, "Can you start Monday?"

"Don't I need to interview with the principal or the teacher?" I asked.

"I am sure they will be very pleased with you," she responded.

Alrighty then. I asked about pay and benefits. They would pay me $8 an hour (yes, really), and I would be eligible to enroll in benefits after ninety days. I reminded myself that the pay did not have to be great—or even good—since the medical benefits were our real priority. Besides, I would contribute to the greater good by educating some of our most vulnerable children. I was doing my part to save the world.

Given such a naively optimistic outlook, what could possibly go wrong?

I was the para in not one but three preschool classes, each with fifteen three- and four-year-olds, including breakfast and lunch duty every day. Forty-five little lives, twenty-one of whom had special needs, many of whom were not potty trained. The classroom teacher was good, and I was appreciated. However, after her para had been in and out with medical issues for three years, she was understandably on the verge of a nervous breakdown. In fact, she was out thirty-five of my first seventy days.

When I had survived what was quite possibly the hardest job I ever had for three months, I called human resources to ask about signing up for health insurance. That was when I learned I had to wait ninety *work* days, not ninety calendar days. Ugh.

I was paid a pittance, and I had to wait almost two more months for insurance coverage. By that time, the school year would be almost over. Somehow, I did survive until June 29, the last day of school. Barely. Stubbornness has gotten me a lot of places in life, and it definitely got me into that classroom each and every day. I also genuinely believed those kids needed me.

That precious health insurance, which finally went into effect mid-June, ran through the end of September. It would remain in place until the month after we set sail only if I returned for a second school year.

"Can I really do that for another year?" I asked myself.

I entertained the idea, but Michael simply said, "No."

Only one other time in all the years we've been together had he actually *forbidden* me from doing something. It was when I wanted to have an outdoor wedding in April in Massachusetts—and he was quite right. As usual, it was in my best interest to listen to him.

In six short months, the job had taken a toll—mentally, emotionally, and physically—on me. "You are stressed and exhausted," he reasoned. "If we are going to be ready in August, you need time and energy to pack up the house and help outfit the boat."

As usual, he had some valid points. We decided to reevaluate my work situation at the end of the summer. For a brief moment, though, I basked in the glory that *my* health insurance was saving us almost $1,500 a month for the next three months. Every little bit helped.

With all of our RV and boat projects, the summer of 2013 quickly passed. My hard-won medical insurance would end on September 30 unless I went back for another year with New Bedford Public Schools. I seriously contemplated it—something about the devil you know? Plus, there is that quirky phenomenon where distance can diminish how bad something really was. Michael was firmly against me going back. In the end, I knew he was right, and I sent in my paperwork, declining to return. So much for saving the world. And my health insurance.

A coveted para position opened up in our town. I applied online and was thrilled when I was selected for an interview with Ally's former principal. I just knew this job was the perfect fit for me and my family. However, I really hadn't considered whether I would be the perfect fit for the school. I would have done a good job for the year I worked, but the school would then have to go through the hiring and training process all over again when I left. In the end, though I was sorely disappointed, it really wasn't a surprise that I wasn't selected.

God would provide. He always does.

I shifted my attention to the gargantuan task of purging and packing up our house to move. A few weeks later, a friend from church asked if I was still looking for a job. She was on the Board of Directors for The Schwartz Center, a private special needs school in nearby Dartmouth. She told me they were looking for a temporary part-time human resources generalist. Temporary *and* part-time? Excellent! And it was even in my field.

She introduced me to the CEO by email, which quickly resulted in an interview with the COO and the director of administration, to whom I would report. In fairly short order, they extended an offer, which I accepted. Though perhaps I should have paid more attention to the pregnant pause when I asked, "What makes you think this human resources position is temporary?" I didn't even think to ask if it was really part-time.

My salary still wasn't anything to write home about, though at $15 an hour, it was nearly twice what I made as a para. Plus, I was actually going to be doing a job for which I was experienced, unlike teaching. The big draw, however, was there was no waiting period for benefits. That's right, health insurance on day one!

As crazy as it sounds, I really enjoyed going into the office every day. It was affirming to be back, somewhat in my pre-Ally world, doing something that I knew how to do—and at which I was pretty good. As much as I loved being at home with Ally, I missed the working part of my world for ten years. I missed the camaraderie of coworkers, the intellectual challenges, and the constant learning mode that comes with the ever-evolving world of human resources. And as I prepared for two years of complete unknown, the confidence I felt at work provided a healthy balance.

What I did not miss was the madness of working in human resources for a small company. The job definitely was not part-time. More often than not, my scheduled thirty hours per week turned into forty. Or more. The extra money was nice, but I much to do at home. In ten short months, we had to move out of our house and onto the boat.

I loved my job, my boss, and my coworkers. It was well-known from the beginning that I was a temporary employee, and yet I had a hard time leaving. I anticipated working only through May. However, I did not say my sad "so longs" until the end of July, just four short weeks before our scheduled departure date.

Add $10,000 for each year worked to the kitty, plus a savings of $27,000 for health insurance over eighteen months.

If you are keeping track, our Magic Number was $346,000. The measures outlined above came up to $325,000. The money was definitely coming together, and it looked as if we were really going to pull it off.

CHAPTER 6

INTRODUCING *DOUBLE PINOCLE*

"You cannot cross the sea merely by standing and staring at the water." —Rabindranith Tagore

We closed on our new boat, *Double Pinocle*, in December 2012, less than six months after we started to talk seriously about taking this trip. It was the first time *my* name was on the deed for our boat, as I married into *Wayward*, and there really was no need to change the ownership. With *Ally Cat*, I figured, "In for a penny, in for a pound," as the old British saying goes. In other words, if I was going to take a risk, I might as well go big.

In the spring, as we discussed how to celebrate our tenth anniversary, instead of a long weekend to some warm romantic destination, we decided to fly to Annapolis, launch the boat together and spend the weekend aboard. It would be a bit like camping, as the only items on the boat were those left by the previous owners. We would even have to bring our own sleeping bags.

The launch went exactly as planned, and in very short order, we were tied up in a slip at the boatyard. I was amazed at how easily Michael was able to maneuver our new boat after having only driven her once during the sea trial. He has so many years of experience with boats—years I will never be able to amass—I wondered if I would ever be comfortable at the helm.

What definitely did not go as planned that weekend was the weather. By the end of March, in the mid-Atlantic region, the world should be showing some serious signs of spring. Not in 2013. It was so cold that the boatyard had turned the water to the docks off. Did I mention that the weekend would be a bit like camping? Perhaps I should have said a *lot* like camping—in the winter! The good news was that we were both so excited about our new boat that even inconveniences like freezing temperatures and no running water couldn't dampen our spirits. Romantic, it was not. And it was a really good thing there was a cozy, warm coffee shop just down the street.

In April, when both Ally and I had school vacation, we drove to Annapolis, towing our Thule trailer, to load the boat with enough gear to sail her home in July. Since our plans included selling *Wayward* and *William*, I unloaded everything from both. Our sunroom looked like a home goods store exploded—kitchenware, linens, and storage solutions were everywhere. However, by seeing it all spread out, I was easily able to decide what to take to the new boat, as well as what was to be donated or thrown out.

I sorted through pots and pans, dishes, silverware, utensils, cups and mugs, hot pads and dish towels, bath and beach towels, sheets, pillows and blankets, storage trays and bins, baskets, toiletries, and first-aid supplies. Once sorted, I packed up the surviving items and loaded them onto the trailer. Meanwhile, Michael also collected gear for the boat, much of which came from *Wayward* and *William,* as well. He sorted through tools and spare parts, cleaning supplies, rags and hoses, dock lines, bosun's chairs, sailing gloves, life jackets, backup GPS and handheld compass, plus charts from Annapolis to Cape Cod and an updated *Eldridge Tide and Pilot Book,* also known as the mariner's bible, which has tides and currents for ports from Key West to Nova Scotia.

He planned ahead to make sure he would have what he needed to complete the projects we deemed necessary before sailing from Maryland to Massachusetts in the summer. Since we were driving, we would have a car while we were there. I easily envisioned a trip or two—or twenty—to marine and hardware stores.

On our growing list of things to buy was an inflatable dinghy. However, we were still more than a year away from doing so, as it was likely either a boat show purchase (the New England Boat Show in Boston, the Newport International Boat Show, or the Annapolis Sailboat Show were all contenders) or a purchase from the marine and boat supplier Defender in Connecticut—only a ninety-minute drive from us—during their annual sale the following April.

As luck, or perhaps Neptune, would have it, during Superstorm Sandy in October 2012, an inflatable dinghy washed up on our marsh, complete with a two-horsepower motor. We contacted the harbormaster and marinas in our town to try to find the owner, with no success. Our harbormaster contacted his peers in neighboring towns, as well as across Buzzards Bay in Falmouth, again, with no success. As it was definitely not new or fancy, he suggested its owner might not be looking too hard for it, hoping for an insurance settlement instead, and deemed it ours. No matter; she would be good enough to get us home. Gifts from the sea, indeed!

We deflated the dinghy and plopped her atop everything else we had collected in the trailer, including my kayak, tied it all down, and drove ten hours to Annapolis.

When Michael and I launched the boat in March, we kept her at the boatyard to have some work done. Once this work was completed, we made arrangements to rent a slip up a creek nearby, where she would live until we could bring her home in July. When we arrived in April, she was still in the boatyard. Since the temperatures were finally well above freezing, and the water to the docks was now on, we could give our girl a good scrubbing. Color me crazy, but I love this part. By scrubbing down every inch inside from bow to stern, I completely connect with my boat. And the resulting love fest lasts all the way from launch in the spring until we haul her out in the fall. I discovered this bizarre phenomenon when I first started cleaning *Wayward* for the season, and it appeared to continue with *Double Pinocle* as well.

Now, about that name. *Double Pinocle.* Spelled with an "h," Double Pinochle is a popular North American card game, though not one with which we have any connection. Superstitions aside, we had to change her name. After tossing around names for a while, we narrowed it down to two finalists: *Buzzard* and *Ally Cat. Buzzard* because we live on and do most of our sailing in Buzzards Bay. You didn't think I was talking about my sweet husband, did you? And *Ally Cat* because our daughter Allison's nickname from birth has been Ally, and the new boat is a catamaran, or a cat, for short. We asked friends for input, and by an overwhelming majority, *Ally Cat* was the winner. It's a little clichéd; however, we all liked it a lot. Besides, how many nine-year-olds have a boat named for themselves?

That settled, we were ready to order the lettering. Having never had a catamaran, we had to figure out where we wanted to put her name and hailing port. We finally decided to put *Ally Cat* in two places on the side of the boat: the portside toward the bow and the starboard side toward the stern. We opted for large black easy-to-read letters. We also decided to put her name under the top portside step on the stern, and our hailing port, Mattapoisett, Massachusetts, under the top starboard side step. These we would have to order in a much smaller size, though we were still conscious that it be easy to read. If we put it across the transom, where *Double Pinocle* had been, when the dinghy was up on the davits, neither the name nor hailing port was visible.

I was, and continued to be, amazed at just how many details went into planning this trip.

After a couple of days of cleaning and organizing all the new items we brought aboard, Michael had a couple of boat chores to do that were going to be much easier without Ally and me in the way, so we planned a sightseeing day in Washington, DC, just a forty-five-minute drive away. I was horrified that Ally was nine years old, and I had never shown her around my hometown. In a few hours, I could at least show her the highlights and whet her appetite for really getting to know my city in the fall of 2014, when we spent the first six weeks of our trip there. The thought of living, albeit temporarily, in DC made me giddy!

I posted a message on Facebook, hoping to persuade at least one of my local friends to play hooky for the day. Though I had no luck with the local gang that day, we managed to put together a cookout that evening. And my friend, Kim, a flight attendant for Delta, saw my post and happened to be in town on a layover that day. Say what you want about social media; that day, I loved Facebook! She was staying at a hotel right in DC and had a few hours to spend with us.

We picked her up on our way from Annapolis, and as I pointed out iconic landmarks—Union Station, the United States Capitol, the Supreme Court, the FBI building, all of the incredible Smithsonian museums, The Mall, the Washington Monument, the White House—Kim and I were transported back to 1987. She and her military family had just moved to Virginia, about fifteen minutes from my home in Alexandria. We had met at Virginia Tech, a five-hour drive from DC, and she had not yet had the opportunity to explore her new hometown. We spent a very memorable day over Christmas break as I showed her the highlights of my beloved city. How appropriate that together we shared our city with Ally!

We took a driving tour first, the full length of The Mall from the Lincoln Memorial to the Capitol, around the Tidal Basin, past the Jefferson Memorial, and into Hains Point National Park, where I did *a lot* of running in my twenties. Our timing was perfect as we were able to catch the tail end of the iconic cherry blossoms surrounding Hains Point and the Tidal Basin.

"Wow, that's new (World War II Memorial) and that, too (Martin Luther King Jr. Memorial)," I exclaimed. "Hey, where did *The Awakening* go?"

The Awakening, a seventy-two-foot by fifteen-foot sculpture by J. Seward Johnson Jr. of the Johnson & Johnson pharmaceutical family, is a giant struggling to emerge from the earth. For as long as I could remember, it was at the tip of Hains Point, the twenty-mile mark of the Marine Corps Marathon. Where on earth could it possibly have gone? We discovered the answer the next summer: National Harbor in Prince George's County, Maryland, just across the Wilson Bridge from Alexandria, where it was moved in 2007.

Enough driving; walking is the way to really see DC. We had no problem parking on Constitution Ave, near 15th Street, which put us right next to the White House and smack in the middle of The Mall. We first stopped to honor the sixteen million who served in the armed forces, the more than 400,000 who died, and the millions who supported the World War II effort from the home front. One of Washington's newest monuments, and the first national memorial dedicated to *all* who served, the National World War II Memorial was dedicated in 2004, four years after I moved from the DC area.

We walked along the Reflecting Pool, home to many significant events throughout our history, from Dr. King's famous "I Have a Dream" speech and other civil rights marches to the annual Fourth of July fireworks. It was even featured in the anti-war protest scene in the movie *Forrest Gump* where Forrest and Jenny were reunited. Built in the 1920s, the Reflecting Pool was completely redesigned in 2012 to eliminate the leaks that caused it to lose about half a million gallons of water a week from the city's municipal water supply. Now drawn from the Tidal Basin as the primary water source, the water is treated and filtered, improving its reflecting quality. The dirt paths leading from the World War II Memorial to the Lincoln Memorial, which had eroded due to so many visitors, were also redone and resurfaced to allow for more accessibility. Looking good, DC.

We walked up the iconic steps of the Lincoln Memorial—our sixteenth president and a fierce defender of democracy—and into the immense chamber. Though captivated by the nineteen-foot-tall statue of Abraham Lincoln, we did manage to read both the Gettysburg Address and Lincoln's second inaugural speech, both of which are inscribed in the interior. Did you know there is a typo on the memorial walls? Yep, the word 'FUTURE' in his second inaugural address was accidentally inscribed as 'EUTURE.' And next time you are in DC, check out Lincoln's hands. Do you think he is signing his initials, AL?

After a scrumptious lunch at one of my favorite haunts from my DC days, Old Ebbitt Grill, we said "so long" to Kim. She left, and we headed to Reston for our cookout. First, we had some time to kill, so we decided to throw a Frisbee on the Ellipse in front of the White House.

As we crossed the street after getting the Frisbee out of the car, we saw the strangest thing: DC Police were closing down Constitution Avenue, and tour buses were racing away from the White House. Definitely not something you see every day. Ally and I wondered what was going on, but we couldn't come up with anything plausible.

Several hours later we learned two bombs had been detonated near the finish line of the Boston Marathon, turning the Patriots Day festivities into chaos. The unusual activity we witnessed suddenly made sense. The bombing was immediately classified as a terrorist attack, explaining why the police had closed down the street, and the tour buses, full of White House officials, not tourists, sped away.

After sending some frantic texts to make sure everyone I knew who was running the marathon or in the city cheering on the runners was safe, we returned to our cookout with forced cheerfulness. We were a little distracted, to say the least.

How bizarre it was to host such conflicting emotions: fear and sadness for those affected by the bombing, anger toward the wrongdoers, and joy and excitement as we marched steadily toward our goal of sailing off into the sunset for two years. Not to mention the lovely day and evening we had with old friends. We are capable of feeling such a wide range of emotions, even conflicting ones, at the same time.

Once back in Annapolis, it was *finally* time to sail. We didn't go far that first day, just around the corner to a pretty little cove surrounded by huge, beautifully landscaped homes. There were hundreds of daffodils in bloom on the shore all around us. And we were finally at anchor in our new boat. Ah, a glimpse of the carrot we were chasing!

After finalizing her name and choosing the lettering, we researched how to de-name and rename a boat, preferably without incurring the wrath of Neptune or Aeolus, the lesser-known Roman god of wind. This is where the internet is both a blessing and a curse. Not only were we able to find a script and details for both the de-naming and the renaming ceremonies, we found dozens. Go ahead, Google it. They ranged in superstition levels from: "You will have nothing but bad luck if you defy the gods and change the name" to

"You will be just fine if you perform the ceremonies properly, with due respect and plenty of alcohol" to "You can go below and mumble the words to yourself."

Not being overly superstitious, but definitely not wanting to anger the gods and bring bad luck (we were going to live on this boat for two years, after all), we agreed to change her name with a proper ceremony performed with reverence. And plenty of alcohol. Armed with the proper scripts and libations, we were ready.

Ally tediously removed *Double Pinocle's* letters from the transom, and we made an effort to remove anything with that name per our de-naming instructions. Luckily, the former owners were not into having the boat name on everything—cups, mugs, dishes, towels, etc.—so this step was not difficult. Next up: the de-naming ceremony. Since the instructions for the ceremonies state they are to be read with flair, and Michael always says I do flamboyant well, he nominated me to serve as mistress of ceremonies. As captain, he, of course, would be responsible for the libations. First, we blessed the former name, and then we asked to erase *Double Pinocle* from the Ledger of the Deep and Neptune's memory. Done. Oh, yes, we had to pour the champagne. Ally had a lot of fun with our ceremony, too.

Given there was no clear agreement that a twenty-four-hour waiting period was required after the de-naming ceremony, apparently to rid the boat of persistent demons, we proceeded directly to the renaming, or christening, ceremony. Besides, we were all on the bow with champagne; it seemed as good a time as any. Again, with flair, I sought blessings for the vessel under her new name, *Ally Cat*, and

INTRODUCING Double Pinocle

all who sailed within. Lacking royalty to perform the honors, our esteemed captain poured the champagne—an entire bottle—over *Ally Cat's* bow. More champagne was poured, and we all toasted again.

The next day, filled with anticipation, we applied the *Ally Cat* and Mattapoisett, MA, lettering to the stern of the boat. We waited to apply the port and starboard lettering until she was out of the water in hopes of getting it on straight.

If you Google de-naming and renaming a boat, *please* do not tell me about the metal tag with the old name written on it in water-soluble ink that should have been dropped from the bow of the boat at the end of the de-naming ceremony. Nor do I wish to be informed, by you detail-oriented folks, that we had items with the new name on board before we completed the de-naming ceremony. I know we were tempting fate. I am a details person, but one can only keep track of so many details at once. Besides, we drank a lot of champagne, which I believe made up for forgetting that stinkin' metal tag. And though I won't ruin the ending, we did enjoy nothing but good luck, so I am going to call both the de-naming and the renaming ceremonies successful.

89

CHAPTER 7

ALLY CAT COMES HOME

"Man cannot discover new oceans unless he has the courage to lose sight of the shore."—Andre Gide

As the summer of 2013 approached, Ally was wrapping up third grade, and it appeared as if I would actually survive my stint as a para in New Bedford Public Schools. In July, we flew to Annapolis and sailed the newly christened *Ally Cat* home. Piling into our rental car, we noted that we had witnessed an entire year of seasons in Annapolis. Our reconnaissance missions started in the fall of 2012, culminating in a family trip to meet *Ally Cat*, nee *Double Pinocle*, the day after Thanksgiving. In December, we completed the survey and sea trial and closed on *Ally Cat*. And though it felt more like the dead of winter than spring, Michael and I celebrated our tenth anniversary and launched *Ally Cat* in March, followed by our April drive to Annapolis to load and rename our girl. Finally, on a ridiculously hot summer day, we arrived in Annapolis to sail *Ally Cat* home to Massachusetts.

Did I mention it was hot? It was definitely way too hot to be tied up to a dock. We decided to move *Ally Cat* out into the bay in hopes of finding a breath of breeze at anchor. One of the benefits of anchoring is that, unless there is strong current, the boat faces into the wind. This allows whatever breeze is blowing to flow through the boat, often providing much-needed relief from the heat. When a boat is tied to a dock, she and the crew are at the mercy of the wind direction.

If the wind is blowing in the wrong direction, with no airflow, the boat can become stifling.

We sailed across the Chesapeake Bay, passing the Naval Academy for the last time in the "Buying-Our-Boat" portion of this adventure. I continued to be in awe of Michael's skills at the helm as we docked at a marina under the Chesapeake Bay Bridge to fuel up for the first time. So many firsts! As a kid, I crossed that span by car dozens of times. Then, we knew we only had two more hours until we were home. Aboard *Ally Cat* that day, our entire adventure before us, our little Crew of Three was headed into very little that was known.

We had a glorious sail up to the northernmost part of the bay. There were thunderstorms all around us, which is not unusual in the Chesapeake on a hot summer afternoon. Keeping a close eye on them, it looked as if the one ahead was going to miss us. Uh oh. Wind direction change.

"We have to get that screecher down," Michael warned.

I took over the helm as Michael prepared to roll the sail up.

"The line is jammed. I'm going up front," he said as he rushed past me.

Plan B: Once on the bow, Michael brought the screecher down by releasing the halyard and tackling the enormous sail as it descended. He grabbed it by armfuls to keep it out of the water, rolling and tucking it any way he could. After he secured the screecher to the foredeck with some extra line, we proceeded up the Bohemia River and anchored without incident in the pouring rain.

Safely at anchor, we could enjoy the rest of the thunderstorm.

"Join me for a Dark 'n' Stormy?" Michael is so calm, even when things do not go as planned. And he is quickly able to shift gears to an alternate idea whenever necessary.

"Why, yes, please," I chirped, grateful for our experienced captain.

Ally, too young to help in the midst of a tense situation, watched intently. Michael does not yell and he does not panic, perhaps two of his finest traits. And also two of the most important attributes for the crew aboard any boat. And she also saw me, with far less experience, default to my captain.

We exited the Chesapeake Bay the following day via the Chesapeake and Delaware Canal, accompanied by another thunderstorm. With no sails up, it was not a problem. Down the Delaware River and through the Cape May Canal, we finally dropped anchor at 3 a.m. Luckily, the top of our mast is only forty-six feet off the water, so we were able to go through the Cape May Canal rather than taking the longer route around.

Cape May. Long-forgotten memories flooded back of taking the paddle-wheel-powered ferry on our way to the Jersey Shore when I was Ally's age. Never could I have imagined all those years ago I would be back, and in my very own boat.

As we sailed *Ally Cat* to Massachusetts, my new favorite quote, courtesy of Suzanne Giesemann, from her book, *It's Your Boat Too: A Woman's Guide to Greater Enjoyment on the*

Water, was, "The difference between an adventure and an ordeal is attitude." My attitude, that is.

I had my first adventure in Cape May. I had not yet passed Dinghy Driver's Ed, so I set out in my kayak to stock up on fruits and vegetables while everyone else was still asleep. We arrived the night before, well after midnight, so I did not have a good lay of the land. What looked like a park the night before, and therefore easy access to shore, was actually a Coast Guard base, so there was no access. I paddled across the channel to the fuel dock.

"Can you please point me in the direction of a grocery store?" I inquired.

"There is a Wawa at the main harbor."

So, I paddled back across the channel and upwind where he pointed. I was getting a great workout, and I figured the paddle home would be downwind.

I finally found the Wawa. Note: Wawa is not a grocery store; it is a convenience store, like a 7-Eleven or a Cumberland Farms. Once we left the States, there were many days when finding a store like that would have made me giddy, but I wasn't there yet. I was still in United States grocery store mode, where an entire aisle was dedicated to breakfast cereals and all of the other opulent choices we take for granted every day. For that, I needed to take a taxi.

The cab driver was delightful, sharing history, lore, and lots of other information about his town. He suggested a walk—about three blocks of shops and restaurants with a pedestrian promenade blocking off the vehicle traffic. I found an old-fashioned five-and-dime store, where I bought

ALLY CAT COMES HOME

water shoes, some medication for seasickness (Ally's, not mine, thankfully), shampoo, swim shirts for all, and even neon-orange nail polish. Orange was Ally's color du jour. My grocery shopping completed—I hadn't started using the cruising term "provisioning" yet—I took a cab back to my kayak, loaded the groceries, and paddled back to *Ally Cat*.

I learned several valuable lessons that day, not the least of which was that my positive attitude is what made it a fun adventure versus an exhausting and frustrating ordeal. I also learned that cruising guides are a necessity as local information is invaluable. Had I researched Cape May as an anchorage in one of the numerous guidebooks available, I would have known where I could easily get ashore, as well as where I would find essentials such as groceries, laundry, banks, post office, propane refills, plus the ever-necessary marine and hardware stores. Not all guidebooks are created equally; however, most will generally give you a better clue than I had that day. Apparently, it was time to start the list of charts, cruising guides, and other reference materials we would need. (See Appendix B.)

In hindsight, I now see that this experience was very much how shopping would be once we left the States. I learned that cruisers do not *grocery shop*, they *provision*. It took me a long time to figure out how to describe the difference. At home, when I shop, generally for food or household items, I make a list and go to the store, maybe two (a superstore or the grocery store and the drugstore, for example). Often, I know my way around the store and can generally pick up almost every item on my list in a single trip.

Provisioning is very different. Yes, I still made the list; in fact, we kept a running list going of items we needed. We were perpetually on the lookout for stores, and we bought things as we found them, oftentimes in random and unplanned locations—and almost always as part of an adventure, which sometimes turned into an ordeal.

By the way, there was a wind shift while I was ashore, and it was an upwind paddle all the way back to *Ally Cat*. It was definitely *all* about *my* attitude.

In late October 2012, Superstorm Sandy, the largest Atlantic hurricane on record, roared through New Jersey and New York at high tide, leaving a path of destruction in its wake. We toyed with the idea of stopping along the New Jersey shore to visit with friends; however, in the end, the weather dictated our plans. In fact, in our efforts to be safe and comfortable, the weather *always* dictated our plans. We had a short weather window, and it was in our best interest to sail from Cape May all the way up the Jersey coast to Sandy Hook, near New York City, in one fell swoop. This one-shot run would also eliminate any uncertainty about what may or may not still be closed after the storm. Additionally, although *Ally Cat* is a very shallow draft boat (she only draws three feet with rudders and sonic outdrive leg down, five feet with the centerboards all the way down, and twenty inches with everything up), we had concerns about charted depths versus actual depths following the hurricane. This was long before we discovered the ActiveCaptain app, an online interactive cruising guide that provided a tremendous source of up-to-date local information for cruisers written by cruisers.

This would be the longest passage so far for our Crew of Three, at eighty nautical miles—a little over seventeen hours—and our first overnight sail.

Since I can sleep just about anywhere, anytime, I volunteered for the midnight to 4 a.m. shift. After enjoying dinner underway, I went to bed at seven, leaving Michael on watch. He woke me five hours later, bribing me with a fresh pot of coffee in the French press. After briefing me on his watch—a situation report that included nearby boats and other lights, our course, necessary adjustments, and any other pertinent information — he fell into bed while I took over the watch.

What does it mean to stand watch? While on watch, I am responsible for the boat and the crew. I am on the lookout for anything or anyone in our way and to make sure we are on course to our destination. I monitor the VHF radio, tuned to Channel 16, the fuel levels and engine temperature, as well as depth, wind speed and direction, and our speed. If sail adjustments are necessary or we have a squall in our path, I wake Michael up to help.

Wildwood, Avalon, Sea Isle City, Beach Haven, Atlantic City—I loved being able to put some of my new navigational skills to use as I continued to learn how to use the GPS and autopilot to stay out of the way of the barges. I was pretty proud of myself: my very first solo watch on my very first overnight sail. Me, the gardener!

Is the engine sputtering? I woke at 8 a.m. to unwelcome engine noises. Almost to Sandy Hook, we were either out of fuel or what was left was too gunky to run the engine. We had spare diesel on board in a jerry can, so Michael added about a gallon to the tank, enough to make it to Horseshoe Cove in Sandy Hook, drop the anchor, and go to sleep—after adding "fuel polisher" and "remove and clean both fuel tanks" to our lists.

Once we were a little more rested, we set out to get diesel. We headed across Sandy Hook Bay to Atlantic Highlands Municipal Marina, the largest public marina on the East Coast. We hoped their fuel dock was operational again following Superstorm Sandy; otherwise, we would have to walk to the nearest service station in town and carry our jerry cans, full of diesel, back to the dinghy to deliver to *Ally Cat*. Over and over. There were sailboats on moorings, which was a good sign, though there were also construction cranes and remnants of pilings, with no sign of the docks that once were attached.

We found the fuel dock, where workers were actively working on the unfinished building. It did not look good; then a fuel attendant emerged and told us they were, in fact, open and they had diesel. Yea! We arrived on a Thursday; they had reopened the Saturday before. My dad had the perfect saying: "I'd rather be lucky than good."

Frustrated with my inability to take the dinghy to shore in Cape May, which led to my kayaking adventure, I finally asked Michael to teach me how to operate the dinghy. Eager to start Dinghy Driver's Ed, knowing the freedom it would allow me, he had been patiently waiting for me to ask. Ally was already miles ahead of me, and she was also getting pretty good at rowing the inflatable—a skill I also needed to master. Dinghy engines are notoriously ornery.

Rather than heading out the next day, we decided to take the day off. On a whim, we took the ferry into New York City. Arriving at Pier 11, we fueled up on bagels, naturally, and walked to the Battery, where we bought tickets to Liberty Island to see the Statue of Liberty up close.

Liberty Island sustained significant damage in Hurricane Sandy, and had just reopened the week before in time for the Fourth of July festivities. There, our good luck ran out as we were thwarted in our efforts to go up the crown or even the pedestal. Those tickets, we were told, sold out weeks in advance. Perhaps months.

We had a great time anyway and enjoyed learning the history and lots of trivia about Lady Liberty and Ellis Island. Do you know what the seven points of her crown signify? The seven continents and the seven seas. Having just studied the continents the year before, Ally was thrilled to recite them for us. So, what are the seven seas? Our first homeschool assignment: research what constitutes the seven seas. We also learned that the tablet in the statue's hands reads, "July 4, 1776," along with many other fun facts. This excursion provided the inspiration for Ally's Halloween costume that year, definitely her best yet: Lady Liberty.

We took a cab up the FDR to 24th and Madison to meet a friend for lunch. Boy, did we look out of place in our beachy clothes among all those businessmen and women in Midtown. We walked up Broadway and through Herald Square. Ally got such a thrill walking past *the* Macy's of the Macy's Thanksgiving Day Parade and standing in the spot where our beloved Rockettes perform every year.

We walked to the Empire State Building and took the elevator to the 86th-floor observation deck, where we felt as if we were on top of the world. Cloud cover had kept it cool all afternoon after a beautiful sunny morning. When it started to mist a little, given the wind, it actually felt cool eighty-six stories high. Who would have thought we'd be chilly in New York City in July?

We continued our walk into Times Square. Lights, lights everywhere. We loved the new walking promenades, as we could easily gawk without worrying about getting run over. One of Ally's friends told her about a huge toy store in Times Square that had a Ferris wheel inside. I mistakenly thought she must be referring to FAO Schwarz, the toy store of my youth, which soared in popularity after the 1988 movie *Big*, starring Tom Hanks. I had been captivated by the life-sized stuffed animals and the floor piano that you could actually play by stepping on the keys. However, it was located on Fifth Avenue, near Central Park, not in Times Square.

Silly me, the three-level 45,000-square-foot FAO Schwarz on the Upper West Side was old news. Located in the new family-friendly Times Square, with four stories and 110,000 square feet, this Toys 'R' Us, had it all. In addition to the sixty-foot-tall indoor Ferris wheel, we found softball gloves, crayons, markers, books, and a motorized scooter, plus thousands of other wonders. There was a Häagen-Dazs ice cream shop and a Wonka candy shop, complete with Nerds, Everlasting Gobstoppers, Laffy Taffy, Sweetarts, and Pixy Stix. Oh, my, what fun!

Completely worn out after a full day exploring New York City, we took the ferry back to Atlantic Highlands and back to the decidedly low-tech island-like cocoon of *Ally Cat*. We moved the boat back over to Horseshoe Cove on Sandy Hook to explore the national recreation area before heading north. The bounty of treasures—mostly sea glass, but some shells, too—we found on the beach were thrilling. Ally found her first piece of rare cobalt-blue sea glass! Michael found an extra-large thick piece of green, and I found a big piece of turquoise, my favorite color. We wondered if Hurricane Sandy, in addition to the brutal destruction it brought to the Northeast, might also have washed some of these treasures ashore. Ally and I have always loved searching beaches for interesting shells and bits of sea glass, and we were eager to comb every single beach in the Bahamas and Eastern Caribbean.

The next day we headed into New York Harbor.

"Look!" Ally exclaimed as the Statue of Liberty came into view. "Wicked cool." I cannot recall the number of times nine-year-old Ally repeated that quintessential Massachusetts saying over the next hour, though I do know it would take more than my ten fingers.

If you have never sailed past the Statue of Liberty on your very own boat, it *needs* to be added to your bucket list. The occasion really called for a cocktail toast, though it was not yet nine in the morning, and we had a lot of miles ahead of us (and our rule is no alcohol while the boat is underway), so Michael and I clinked our coffee mugs in celebration.

Dodging the Staten Island Ferry, not to mention several barges and statue cruises, we gazed in awe at the iconic view stretching before us. Minus the Twin Towers, once the defining symbol of the New York City skyline, it always appears awkward to me.

"There are so many boats out here! How does everyone stay out of everyone else's way?" Ally wondered.

"Just like there are rules we have to follow when we're driving a car, there are rules of the road for boats, too," I responded, fresh from my navigation course.

"Rules of the road for boats? But there are no roads out here!" Ally laughed.

"There is a whole set of rules boats have to follow," Michael added. "The Coast Guard has an entire book dedicated to them."

"When we go through our *Sailing Skills and Seamanship* book next year, we will be learning those rules," I explained. "Did you know all motorboats are supposed to give way to us, as a sailboat, when we are under sail, but as soon as we turn on the engine, we become a motor boat and have to follow the rules for when two motor boats meet."

"Huh. Who knew?"

We sailed around the Battery, the southern tip of Manhattan Island facing New York Harbor, and up the East River.

"Ally, look! There's the Chrysler Building. And the Empire State Building, where we were yesterday," I pointed out. "See the building with all of the different flags flying outside? That is the United Nations Headquarters."

"Wicked cool!"

I followed along on our paper charts as we went under the Brooklyn, Manhattan, and Williamsburg bridges, with Manhattan off our port side and Brooklyn on our starboard. Ally's favorite perch was in the helm seat next to Michael, where she followed along on our GPS as we continued under the Queensboro Bridge and finally the Triborough Bridge.

After the excitement of the East River, it was a relief to sail into Long Island Sound and drop our anchor in Manhasset Bay in Port Washington. It's a cruisers' paradise: the anchorage was protected from the wind in just about any blow; there was easy access to fuel, water, and a holding tank pump out; I found lovely areas to run; there was an assortment of interesting restaurants; and last, but definitely not least, there was a fantastic grocery store (Stop & Shop), with a liquor store next door, right across the street from the town dock, where we tied up our dinghy. We definitely planned to stop there again on our way south.

Another magnificent sail east through Long Island Sound brought us to the Thimble Islands in Branford, Connecticut, a captivating archipelago of 365 pink granite islands. We took a dinghy tour all around the area and were treated to the most magical sunset. The photo we took, in which Ally's bright orange sun shirt matched the bright orange clouds, graced our Christmas card a few months later.

We spent a couple of days in Old Lyme, Connecticut, with Michael's brother, John, and his family. Ally and her cousins had an absolute blast jumping from *Ally Cat's* highest point, and even I joined in. GoPros were all the rage that summer, and we had fun with videos and still shots all day. In fact, one of the greatest pictures—one of Michael doing a swan dive with a huge grin on his face— made me smile so much that I used it as the background photo on my computer the whole year before we left.

I continued to get dinghy driving lessons and practiced my new skills. Maneuvering boats just was not at all intuitive for me, as it seemed to be for both Michael and Ally. I was so nervous that I barely remembered to breathe. I wondered if I would ever really get the hang of it. I did, however, feel brave enough to shuttle my sister-in-law solo into shore. Progress.

Though we didn't make definitive plans to attend, in the back of our minds, we hoped to join a group of Gemini owners for an informal rendezvous in Three Mile Harbor in East Hampton, New York, the third weekend in July. Amazingly, the timing and location worked perfectly as we made our way toward home.

As my very first "raft-up," where four or five other Geminis were anchored yet tied up to each other, it made for quite the festive occasion. We walked from boat to boat, visiting and sharing drinks and appetizers. It was a great opportunity to talk with and learn from folks who had been sailing Geminis just like *Ally Cat* for years. I was able to see what they did to make their boats feel more like home, how they used the spaces in their galleys, and other clever storage ideas.

Old Man Weather—or is it Mother Nature?—once again ruled supreme. Rather than stay to enjoy the fireworks in Three Mile Harbor on Saturday night, the forecast dictated that we leave a day early. After enjoying such a brief stay with our Gemini brethren, we promised we would come to the annual rally again and stay longer the next time.

True to our word, we did go back. Three years later, as we were heading north on our way home from our two-year trip, we again stopped in Three Mile Harbor to join the rendezvous. Amusingly, that second time, *we* were the seasoned cruisers after living on *Ally Cat* for two years and sailing to Grenada and back.

With the extra day near home, we decided to introduce *Ally Cat* to one of our favorite anchorages: Lake Tashmoo, a 270-acre coastal pond on Martha's Vineyard near Vineyard Haven. We had a *fabulous* twelve-hour sail there from Long Island Sound, with twenty to twenty-five mph winds (gusts to thirty) and five- to seven-foot seas, spaced far enough apart to be comfortable, from behind. And I loved every minute of it—no hanging on for dear life while heeled over seasick.

We were blessed with a relatively uneventful cruise, and on July 22, 2013, we sailed *Ally Cat* into our cove and picked up our mooring. We were welcomed home with yet another gorgeous sunset.

Ally Cat, meet Brandt Island Cove. Brandt Island Cove, meet the newest member of our family, *Ally Cat*.

Looking out our back door and seeing *Ally Cat* on her mooring in our cove for the rest of the summer gave us a daily glimpse of the carrot, providing motivation for the next twelve months of effort that was necessary in order to set sail. It was all becoming so much more real by the day.

We learned a lot about our new-to-us boat during our two-week delivery cruise, sailing from Annapolis to Massachusetts. We also spent as much time on *Ally Cat* as we could manage that summer before her scheduled haul-out in September. We took her out for several day sails and even managed a week on Martha's Vineyard. This gave us more time to learn her ins and outs and to get more comfortable living aboard *Ally Cat*. Generally, we keep our boat in the water until sometime in October unless a storm forces us out earlier. However, with a long list of to-dos at home and on *Ally Cat*, not to mention *Wayward* and *William*, the chances for fall sailing were slim.

In New England, particularly in our little seaside town of Mattapoisett, full of boaters, it is not at all uncommon to see boats—big boats—on stands in the yard next to a home. There are very few traditional neighborhoods with by-laws or town ordinances that prohibit doing so, and frugal Yankees, like my husband, like to save on boat storage and have the freedom to do their own maintenance work. In fact, before we were engaged, Michael made sure I understood that he would always own big boats that required a hydraulic boat trailer to move and a crane to step and unstep the mast.

Though I likely didn't understand all of those terms at the time, I did know that a big truck would drive over our lawn each fall to deposit a boat onto stands in our yard. That same truck would come back in the spring to retrieve it and put it in the water. Giving up any attachment I might develop for the grass on the far side of our house, I agreed to his terms. Not exactly a traditional prenuptial agreement!

We live at the end of a dead-end dirt road, which is actually quite well suited to store boats (where there is one, there are always more) and RVs and trailers. Though a third of our land is under water at high tide, we have a little shy of five acres. In 2010, we cleared about a quarter of an acre for my vegetable gardens, apple trees, a shed, and a greenhouse. While everything was dug up, we ran electricity and water over to the gardens and shed, too. Between the shed and our road, we added enough material to ensure the ground was firm enough to park vehicles. Or boats. Though *William*, the RV, used to live there, *Wayward* moved over, awaiting her spa treatments and the necessary work to get her sold.

The far side of our house, however, is the prime location for a boat on stands. Our house is built up on a cement foundation—what is called "up on stilts" around here—eighteen feet above mean high water, per building codes, to mitigate the risk of flooding. When Michael was building the house, he would check progress frequently. Once the foundation was complete, he realized that getting up to that height eliminated most of the mosquitoes. Not surprisingly, he regularly began to hang out on the foundation, enjoying a beer or two, and watching the sunset. As he was contemplating life one evening, it dawned on him that where he sat was the same height he would be if he were on his boat in the yard on stands.

A light bulb went on. He asked the builder to put in a gate on the far side of the wraparound deck railing. He designed and built a ramp to go from the deck to the boat, and—voila! We are able to walk right from the deck to the boat via the ramp. We no longer needed to go down a flight of stairs from our front door to get to the ground level, then up a rickety ladder to get onto the boat.

We were ready to pull *Ally Cat* out of the water. Often, catamarans are hauled in a marina using what's called a Marine Travelift, or a mobile boat hoist. The boat is moved into a U-shaped well in the water, and the four-wheeled Travelift is moved into position above the boat. Once slings are positioned under the hulls, the boat is lifted out of the water and moved within the boatyard, where it will be stored on stands or blocks.

Since *Ally Cat* was coming to our yard, she had to be lifted out of the water on a road-registered vehicle. With *Wayward* and any other keelboat, Brownell Systems is the answer. Using the hydraulic boat trailer and the adjustable boat stands designed by Fred Brownell, the team at Brownell Systems, located right in our little town, haul and launch hundreds of boats every spring and fall. However, our catamaran was quite the novelty for them.

We researched the manufacturer's specifications to find out where the Gemini can safely be lifted and blocked and marked *Ally Cat's* hull with black grease pencil. Tommy Brownell himself, Fred's son, came to supervise. It was quite nerve-wracking, though we successfully lifted her out of the water.

After waiting patiently for the mast to be unstepped and stored, we drove the five miles from the Town Wharf to Meadowbrook Lane. En route, we took up the entirety of Main Street, both of the westbound lanes on Route 6, and the whole width of Brandt Island Road. No wonder we needed our own "Wide Load" escort truck! After some major pruning along our road, we crossed our fingers and desperately hoped she would fit going down Meadowbrook Lane. She brushed against some of the larger arborvitae at the top of the street; otherwise, it was a complete success.

The final step was to transfer *Ally Cat* from the truck to the 8x8 timbers in our yard and free the truck. It was a very tense hour, though again, it was a success. Michael moved the ramp from the deck into place, and we covered her in shrink wrap to protect her from snow and ice damage over the winter.

Bring on the boat projects.

CHAPTER 8

BOAT PROJECTS AND ONLINE BOYFRIENDS

"There is nothing—absolutely nothing—half so much worth doing as simply messing about in boats." — Kenneth Grahame, The Wind in the Willows

When we were boat shopping, we purposely looked for a pretty simple boat in terms of systems so we could decide on and add our own. In our budget, we included the purchase of all new electronics, a watermaker, and a number of other items. It was easier to select and install everything ourselves without first having to remove old equipment. *Ally Cat* completely fit the bill. She had a small GPS with a four-inch screen, not dissimilar to what we used on *Wayward*, Raymarine's Basic Wind, Speed, and Depth Pack, and a Raymarine autopilot.

Ourselves? Who am I kidding? This is *definitely* not my department. Over the course of nine months, Michael completely redid or added everything on *Ally Cat*: electrical and plumbing systems, electronics, as well as anchoring systems, safety equipment, and miscellaneous boat gear. We sought out a boat with relatively low engine hours, so *Ally Cat's* original Westerbeke engine remained, along with the Raymarine products.

Though Michael came to this party with a lot of knowledge, our new-to-us Gemini 105Mc was new to all of us. To shorten the steep learning curve, Michael joined a group of Gemini owners who shared information in a Yahoo Group, Gemini

Catamarans. Within the group, he was able to read all of the archived posts. This gave him two things: a better idea of what regularly breaks so we could start a good spare parts list, and it also became clear to him who, within the group, really knew what they were talking about. One owner, in particular, stood out: Walt.

Walt *loves* working on his boat. Plus, he is brilliant and enjoys showing and telling what he had done with extremely detailed YouTube videos. Yep, Michael was officially cheating on me with Walt, his insanely knowledgeable online boyfriend! You didn't think *I* was the one with an online boyfriend, did you?

Though "boat works" is not my department, and this really is Michael's chapter, I know there are readers who will not view my story as complete without at least some of the following details. Please note: you will not get *all* of the details here. If you want to learn how to do any of these things, YouTube is your friend. Or you can ask my hubby to write a book! Or perhaps Walt will write *his*.

With that disclaimer, here goes.

Michael's list was long. Lists. Like me, he had multiple lists going; boat projects, things to research, and things to buy were the primary lists. The list of tools and spare parts to bring became important as we got closer to departure. The projects fell into some larger categories: engine, electrical power, electronics, anchoring, freshwater/plumbing, and the wide-ranging miscellaneous, a catch-all for the multitude of projects that defied categorization. Additionally, he kept the list of gear we would bring.

Safety equipment was also on Michael's list. However, that category is so big and so important that it warrants its own chapter. (See Chapter 9: Safety First)

Engine

Ally Cat came with the standard Gemini 105Mc Westerbeke Diesel 27 horsepower Model 30B diesel engine. It is connected to a Sillette sonic outdrive leg. Weighing in at a robust 400 pounds, the engine is mounted under the center cockpit hatch. While a diesel engine was not new to Michael, the Westerbeke was. Michael familiarized himself primarily by poking around on his own, reading the owner's manual and all the archived posts in the Gemini owners' group. However, he also hired a mechanic to do a survey, giving him a tutorial as he went, which was invaluable. As was Walt.

With Walt's generous help, Michael figured out how to remove the outdrive leg, clean and paint it, and put it back together. Based on information he read, it appeared the steering cables would likely need to be replaced at least once during our trip, so he replaced them before we left. And he added "steering cables" to his growing list of spare parts.

Ally Cat has two eighteen-gallon fuel tanks located under the aft deck on either side of the engine. Michael pulled both out and cleaned them. He also figured out how to do basic maintenance, such as changing the oil and fuel filters.

The islands of Hispaniola and Puerto Rico are separated by the Mona Passage, which connects the cold Atlantic Ocean to the much warmer Caribbean Sea. In April 2015, during the most technical sailing we encountered, our trusty

Westerbeke began to sputter more than fifteen hours after we had set sail from Samaná in the Dominican Republic. And then it stopped.

I know, I know. We're a *sailboat,* and we can always *sail.* However, we were about twenty miles off the coast of Puerto Rico, in the lee of the island. This meant we were sheltered from the wind by the island, and therefore, there was very little wind with which to sail.

Our sails were up, the engine silent, as Michael started troubleshooting while *Ally Cat* bobbed. He determined it was a fuel issue. We had enough fuel, which was good news; however, it was not getting to the engine. Michael changed out the fuel filter, thinking it might be clogged. No dice. Finally, he performed fuel bypass surgery. Right in the middle of the Mona Passage. Voila. The Westerbeke, which I had already nicknamed the Westerbeast, was humming again. We motorsailed the last twenty miles into Boqueron on duct tape and prayers.

While plowing through the seemingly unending list of boat projects, as Michael watched Walt's YouTube videos, he became convinced that Walt was local. Even though Walt had taken great pains to keep both his boat's name and their hailing port out of videos, Michael recognized some local landmarks and saw bits and pieces of the hailing port. Sure enough, when Michael asked, we discovered he lived five miles away. Amusingly, we went to church with his parents and sister, and his brother's niece taught Ally piano for two years. What a small, small world it is!

Electrical Power

Not long before deciding to sell *Wayward*, we bought two brand new Mastervolt Slimline 200-volt batteries. We poached them from *Wayward* before selling her, swapping them with the batteries that came with *Ally Cat*. Michael bought and installed a Magnum MM1012E, a 1,000-watt inverter, and 50-amp charger, along with a Balmar alternator and voltage regulator (6 series, 70-amp, single-foot). He also rewired the charging circuits.

When the engine is not running, either while sailing or when we are not underway, the battery still needs to be charged. Foregoing a fossil-fuel-powered generator, which is too noisy for our tastes, our primary source of alternative power was solar, rather than wind or water. We bought a single 270-watt house panel from a local off-the-grid place in Marlborough, Massachusetts. They designed the system with Michael's input and measurements. Since they were just over an hour away from us, we could easily drive there to pick up the panel, the controller, and the other components necessary for installation. Prior to installing the panel, Michael had to build a solar panel mount on the existing dinghy davits.

Electronics

A chartplotter allows us to integrate GPS satellite navigation with nautical charts (which are similar to road maps, but with more information for mariners), allowing us to accurately see where we are and track our speed and direction. It is basically the brains of the boat, as each of the other components transmits data to it. After a significant amount of research, Michael decided to buy the B&G Zeus 12 chartplotter with C-Map. Since we planned to keep *Ally Cat* for many years, we opted to wait for the brand-new touch-screen option. This meant using version 1.0 of the B&G hardware and the software, which was not necessarily ideal; however, ten years down the road, non-touchscreen technology would seem *really* dated.

When it worked, it was tremendous. However, we had many frustrating moments with Zeus (he, too, became part of the family). The good news is B&G's customer service was excellent. The bad news is we had to utilize it twice. They replaced our unit once in North Carolina in November 2014, when the touch screen delaminated, and a second time in St. Martin in May 2015, when the touch screen delaminated again. Literally, the layers peeled off. I guess by the time we installed the new unit in St. Martin, we were no longer on version 1.0.

If we had to do it all over again, we would seriously consider going with GPS-enabled iPads or some other type of tablet and install a mount at the helm station.

The rest of the electronics easily fall into the Safety Equipment category; however, given their electrical nature, I've included them here.

Michael installed B&G's Broadband 4G radar with a large dome, as well as B&G's Automatic Information System (AIS). AIS, required equipment for commercial vessels, is optional for recreational boats. It tracks other vessels equipped with AIS and, using Zeus, displays the name, description, and size of the vessel, and whether they are underway (sometimes these huge cargo ships are anchored in what seems like the middle of nowhere!) plus their speed and course, if they are underway. The system then calculates, given their speed and heading, when and how close the closest point of approach (CPA) will be. AIS is similar to aviation's transponder technology.

There are two types of AIS—"receive only," which allows recreational boaters to see the "big guys," and "transmit and receive," which allows them to see us as well. We opted for the "transmit and receive" version, which means not only do we know who is nearby, but they also know where—and who—we are. Having a name comes in quite handy if you need to call the bridge of a commercial vessel on the radio! Although nothing is better than using our own eyes to see what is around us, there is a lot to be said for the additional information we gained from both radar and AIS.

All of these electronics "talk" to each other, along with the existing Raymarine Wind, Speed, and Depth Pack, and autopilot. Once it's all set up, this multitude of data can be viewed on Zeus's fancy touch screen. When it's working. Of course, creating that network sounds an awful lot easier than it was to accomplish. Thank goodness Michael is both patient and persistent.

The first two weeks of our trip were designated "vacation." In reality, these two weeks were a "shakedown delivery cruise." It was a "shakedown" in the sense that almost every system was new. Given we launched *Ally Cat* two and a half weeks before departure, most of them were largely untested. And it was a "delivery" in that we planned to get both boat and crew from Massachusetts to Washington, DC, during those two weeks.

A mere six days in—our first full day in the Chesapeake Bay—we scooted up the Bohemia River in Maryland just before a summer thunderstorm blew through. We were snug as bugs on *Ally Cat*, fittingly enjoying Dark 'n' Stormy cocktails in the cockpit, watching it pour. Just as we were toasting our good timing, we heard the loudest crack of thunder I had ever heard, almost simultaneously timed with a flash of lightning. This cell was literally right over us. I shrieked as the hair stood up on my neck. Interestingly, it wasn't until four days later that our autopilot and the wind, speed, and depth pack—basically the only original electronics—started acting squirrely. We apparently had what was called a near-miss lightning strike—not a direct hit but in close enough proximity to cause damage to our electronics. Once we were in DC, we replaced these with the same Raymarine products, just the new models.

There I go with the "we" again. I am a real comedian. Actually, since Michael was still working full time to wrap up his project, and we filed an insurance claim, we did something we rarely do; we hired one of our new dock neighbors, a marine electrician, to do the work.

A marine VHF (very high frequency) radio is basically a telephone on board, allowing us to communicate with other boats, marinas, bridges, and the coast guard within twelve to twenty miles, depending on conditions. It is a virtual lifeline. We purchased and Michael installed the iCom VHF with a remote mic. Our VHF is in the most logical place on *Ally Cat*, which is just above the electrical panel as you enter the salon to the left; however, this is four to five steps from the helm station in the cockpit. We decided a remote mic was the way to go, with a mount both inside and outside at the helm station, so we would have a full VHF operation at the helm station in plain view of Zeus and his multitude of data.

In addition to the stationary VHF radio aboard *Ally Cat*, Michael also purchased a portable handheld VHF. The portable goes in the dinghy any time she is deployed. Here again, the portable is a lifeline to help. It is also useful while we are on land to communicate back to *Ally Cat*, as in "Ground Control to Major Tom" and "Houston, we have contact."

We had a receiver to tune into Marine Weather Center Chief Forecaster Chris Parker's daily weather reports. The reception was pretty sketchy in the Bahamas; however, we also paid to receive his forecasts via email. Once we made it to the Caribbean, we were able to tune in much more easily.

Anchoring

A significant piece of safety equipment aboard *Ally Cat* is our anchoring setup, collectively referred to as ground tackle. Michael likes big anchors. I cannot lie. For *Ally Cat*, we purchased both a Rocna 20 and a Fortress FX16. The Rocna is our main anchor, with 150 feet of chain and 150 feet of 5/8" 8-plait line. We have two additional anchor rodes that are a combination of line and chain.

Though definitely on the "nice to have" list, we opted for an automated anchor windlass for the first time. Though the boat and all of the systems were new to us, even the idea of a windlass, versus a manual winch, to raise and lower the anchor was novel. And before you get any ideas, *I* was not the "winch" on *Wayward*! Our windlass has a hardwired switch at the helm, meaning we can raise and lower the anchor from the cockpit, which allows for single handing. However, with the remote, I can be at the helm, adding forward or reverse as needed, while Michael is up front on the bow with the remote, raising or lowering the anchor and managing the chain coming in or going out of the anchor locker. Pretty fancy and very civilized!

Plumbing and Fresh Water

The port side of *Ally Cat*, where the navigation station is located, served as an electrical shop from the time the boat was hauled in 2013 until we launched her in 2014, just before tossing the dock lines. Similarly, on the starboard side, my galley (also known as the kitchen) was temporarily a plumbing shop. Before setting sail, Michael replaced all of the hoses in the head (also known as the bathroom) and rebuilt the head pump, replacing the seals, valves, O-rings, and other components located inside the head's hand pump. It wasn't the last time he had to rebuild the head, but I will say we never had a problem with our head smelling. Go Michael!

Ally Cat has two thirty-gallon freshwater tanks, one each located under the quarter berth bunks. Conserving fresh water is almost always a *thing* on a boat. Though it was not a necessity, nor did it relate to our safety, we budgeted for a water maker, so we were not perpetually planning our trip around finding fresh water. Using reverse osmosis, the Spectra Ventura 200T Desalinator system we purchased, and Michael installed, produces a little more than eight gallons an hour, filtering out more than 99 percent of the salt. With our freshwater freedom, Michael added a shower fixture on the port steps to rinse off after swimming.

Michael also installed a salt water wash down on the bow, another nice-to-have.

Miscellaneous Boat Projects

Most of our sailing would be warm-weather sailing, and frequently hot-weather sailing. We did not have the luxury of air conditioning aboard *Ally Cat*, so we were quite keen to keep her as cool as possible. One of our most significant upgrades in this area was the full cockpit enclosure we had made. This was *such* a great idea, as it gave us basically an extra room, which was either a sunroom or a lanai, depending on the weather. With a combination of canvas and clear plastic that rolled up or could be removed to encourage airflow, we basically added another third to the amount of living space, which is pretty significant on a thirty-four-foot boat.

Ally Cat has four large hatches—two in the salon and one each in our master berth and the head—that allow a delicious breeze to flow through the boat when we are at anchor and the wind is blowing. We added shade covers to each of the hatches to stop the sun from beating in and heating up the entire boat.

One of the most charming features of sailing in the eastern Caribbean is the frequent rain, particularly during the rainy season from May to November. Although we adopted the local term from Dominica, "liquid sunshine," and it never seemed to last very long or interfere with our plans, it posed a dilemma with our four big hatches if we wanted to stay cool *and* dry. Enter hatch hoodies, which are essentially umbrellas for the hatch. We bought two, one for each of the front hatches. These small pieces of canvas, with attached lines, allowed us to keep at least two hatches open all the time while we were at anchor. This eliminated the necessary fire drill of rushing below to close all the hatches when it started to rain, as well as racing back to *Ally Cat* from shore for that fire drill.

Painting the inside of all of the lockers was also on Michael's "Miscellaneous" list. If you have never spent much time on a boat, you may not know this is a big project, one more suited for a cast member from Cirque du Soleil than the average human. Suffice it to say, yoga and pilates classes are good training for doing just about anything in any locker. I am not at all sure how he did it, but Michael somehow convinced my sweet uncle this would be fun and a good project they could work on together. After all, Uncle Walter had been offering his help for months. Are we having fun yet?

My beloved salon table was in the house in Michael's office, on its umpteenth iteration of being refinished. Michael struggled mightily with this, specifically with how long it took to dry. When the table was flat to dry, dust particles from the air settled on it and created bubbles. When he tried tilting it sideways to dry, the epoxy slid, creating drip marks. He sanded and finished that table half a dozen times. He tried two different two-part epoxies, one that he brushed on and one that he sprayed on. After the final sanding, he ended with one coat of Epifanes in a beautiful matte finish that looked great and held up remarkably well throughout our two years of steady use and even abuse. In hindsight, Michael said he would have put on one more coat of the Epifanes, but that task just didn't make the cut before it was time to go.

Gear for *Ally Cat*

With a little instruction and practice, any one of the three of us was able to operate the dinghy, giving us precious freedom to escape *Ally Cat* when need be. However, with three crew members, we wanted three ways off the boat.

I am much more comfortable in my kayak than I am at the helm of any motorized vessel, and I love the solitude and independence that paddling on my own provides. When running, hiking, and bicycling aren't options, kayaking, yoga, and swimming are my go-to activities for exercise. For me, regular exercise equals sanity.

We bought an Ocean Kayak Tetra 10. My 10-foot 8-inch kayak, made of incredibly durable polyethylene, weighs in at a relatively light forty-seven pounds. It's heavier than fiberglass or marine-grade plywood; however, it's tough. It's also stable, especially for a "sit-on-top" style, and easy to maneuver. I'm particularly fond of Ocean Kayak's Comfort Hybrid seat, which is padded on the back and bottom, and the adjustable foot pegs. Plus, it fits well when tied to the stanchions on *Ally Cat's* front deck.

Though I occasionally shared my kayak (named *Li'l Cat* or *Scat*, depending on who you asked), Michael and Ally's preferred escape was the inflatable stand-up paddle board (iSUP). Santa left a Tower Adventurer I under our tree for Christmas 2013. As we were all new to paddle boarding, we chose one that was affordable, stable, and inflated quickly. It's 9 feet, 10 inches long, and weighs in at twenty pounds. Deflated and rolled up with the fin removed, it fits into a large duffle bag. Though we tried to avoid storing the iSUP in direct sunlight, when we were not on a long passage and using it frequently, we often kept it inflated up on the front deck, too. Ah, the joys of a 14-foot-wide catamaran.

Before we left the States in December 2014, we ventured to Divers Direct, a large dive store in West Palm Beach, Florida for snorkel gear. We each got outfitted with wetsuits, masks, snorkels, fins and swim shirts. Michael, our hunter, added weight belts, gloves, pole spears, and mesh bags for the fish he would surely catch to our growing pile, as we hoped to enjoy some culinary gifts from the sea. With a giant mesh backpack to hold it all, we were ready for underwater adventures, and anxious for that celebrated crystal-clear turquois water in the Bahamas. Four hours and about $1,200 later, we were ready.

While we were in West Palm Beach, we also stopped into Gander Mountain Sports, where we supplemented our fishing gear with some new rods, reels, and lures. I decided to experiment with cast iron cookware, finding a small Lodge two-quart covered seasoned cast iron serving pot in the camping section. The size was perfect for our little oven and was versatile enough to go from stovetop to oven. My cornbread, already a fan favorite, came out even better in that pan.

I'll admit it right now: I am camera-challenged. For me, durability is the number one feature I look for in a camera. Before we left, I had an Olympus Tough. It was waterproof, dustproof, shockproof, crushproof, anti-fogging, and freeze-proof. (I hoped not to test that last feature on our trip.) Still, we had to replace it once during our trip. Even though I love to take pictures and even have a pretty decent eye for a good shot, neither Michael nor I are good at taking videos. When we were expecting Ally, we bought a four-door car and a camcorder because that's what we thought we were *supposed* to do. Though the car decision made life with an infant car seat much more tolerable, I can probably count on two hands the number of times we used the camcorder.

Michael did buy a GoPro, all the rage in 2013, along with a bunch of accessories. I am pretty sure I can count on two hands the number of times he used that, too. Apparently, we are much more interested in being in the moment than documenting those moments via video. So, while we won't be starring on any YouTube channels anytime soon—at least as filmmakers—we did come back with some stunning photos. A lot of them.

In order to include photos in this book, either the print or digital format, I had to agree to a black-and-white presentation. Sadly, that proved very dissatisfying to me as a photographer. Instead, I will sort through the more than 10,000 shots and post the best on my blog at https://kimberlyjwardwriter.com/blog/

CHAPTER 9

SAFETY FIRST

"An ounce of prevention is worth a pound of cure." —
Benjamin Franklin

On *Ally Cat*, safety comes first, second, and third.

The coast guard provides the federally mandated minimum equipment requirements in the United States. These are based on boat length (under 16 feet, 16-26 feet, 26-40 feet, and over 40 feet), which, for us at 34 feet, include life jackets, fire extinguishers, visual distress signals, and sound-producing devices. We easily met these minimum standards, and then exceeded them.

We carry with us a half a dozen of the standard orange Type II life vests, three of which live in the dinghy. We have three Class B fire extinguishers aboard *Ally Cat* and one in the dinghy, exceeding the minimum requirements. And we carry the requisite three day/night flares, unexpired, and a horn that is audible for half a mile.

Lin and Larry Pardey wrote a book called *The Self Sufficient Sailor* in 1982. The title says it all. While cruising, self-sufficiency is the most basic tenet. From fuel supply to fresh water, oil changes to steering cable replacement, solar panel maintenance to first aid, food provisions to homeschooling plans and implementation, what we ourselves were capable of was the difference between an adventure and an ordeal.

We were our own self-sufficient village on board our thirty-four-foot *Ally Cat*. As creative problem solvers, we managed it all.

However, in the unlikely event that a situation surpassed our ability to manage it, we had a failsafe—an EPIRB. This Emergency Positioning-Indicating Radio Beacon sends out a global distress signal for help, if needed. It is basically a 911, or SOS, call.

Interestingly, though many believe SOS stands for Save Our Ship or even, a bit more accurately, Save Our Souls, it is not an acronym. The letters don't stand for anything at all. It is simply a Morse Code string of three dots, three dashes, and three dots (...---...) with no spaces or stops. Originally used by Germany and adopted by the International Radio Telegraphic Convention in 1906, it was agreed upon as the universal distress signal because it can be sent quickly and easily. It is also hard to misinterpret.

The EPIRB is a battery-powered radio transmitter that is both watertight and buoyant. We have an ACR 406 MHz Category 2 EPIRB on board *Ally Cat*. When activated, it triggers a worldwide search-and-rescue network, utilizing an encoded signal transmitted via satellite. We registered it when we purchased it, so the signal includes who we are, *Ally Cat's* pertinent information, our location, and our emergency contact information. It does not hurt that our emergency contact, my sister Stacie, is a retired United States Coast Guard captain.

Activating the EPIRB is a last resort. We would only do that after every other option has been exhausted. It is meant to save our crew if *Ally Cat* is sinking and/or get assistance for a life-threatening medical emergency. Once activated, we must be ready to abandon ship.

While it is impossible to be prepared for every single situation that can go wrong, it is possible to run through a number of worst-case scenarios and determine a plan for each one. Additionally, any time we read about or hear about a tragedy at sea, instead of adding it to our list of fears, we, as a family, deconstruct what happened and consider how we could and would react in each scenario. One of the biggies is a man (or woman) overboard.

The first rule on *Ally Cat*, and it is quite simple, is to stay on the boat.

For anyone who chooses not to follow rule number one, rule number two is to stay with the boat. To this end, in addition to the traditional orange life vests, we each have a Mustang Survival self-inflating personal flotation device (PFD) with a harness. Each is adjusted specifically for our body and fits perfectly. They each have two stainless steel D-rings on the harness to which we attach our tethers. Tethers are exactly what they sound like: they attach us by way of our harness to *Ally Cat*. In the cockpit, we clip onto the helmsman chair. Anytime we leave the cockpit, we clip onto one of the jacklines.

Jacklines, which are webbing straps, are attached to *Ally Cat* across our back deck. Additionally, they run from the stern to the mast and from the mast to the bow on both the port and starboard sides. Jacklines allow us to remain attached to the boat while moving from side to side along *Ally Cat's* transom as we visually take in our surroundings. Or when the captain relieves himself off the stern steps. We can also safely move from the cockpit up onto the front deck to deal with sail issues or whatever else may be necessary. We use a double tether, enabling us to move the second tether to another spot while still clipped on with the first. We are always attached to *Ally Cat*, thereby following rule number two.

For crew who insist on disregarding these rules, you are just being ornery. Please see the captain for an attitude readjustment. If you *are* the captain, please see the admiral.

If one of us chooses to go for an unplanned swim without being attached to *Ally Cat*, the very best chance for survival is to be rescued by the remaining crew aboard. By discussing our man overboard procedures while at anchor, and even at the dinner table on land, and by practicing man overboard drills both in a calm bay and under more difficult circumstances, we have developed the skills to enact a rescue, if necessary.

Some additional equipment helps, too. We have a man overboard pole, consisting of a rod with a flag, a horseshoe buoy, and a light. This is used to mark the position of the man overboard. We also have two throwable cushions, allowing us to get more things in the water to help keep sight of the man overboard. It's surprisingly easy to lose a person in the water. Since we are a crew of three, it is one person's responsibility to maintain visual contact and point at the man overboard the entire time.

We have a whistle tied to each of our PFDs, and both a marine laser light and a safety knife tucked into the small front zipper pocket. We attached a Mustang accessory pocket to the waist band of each of our PFDs for our individual survival equipment: a personal locator beacon (PLB) and a personal AIS transmitter, which enables those on *Ally Cat*—using Zeus's beautiful screen—to see where the man overboard is located.

Our Marine Boating Lifesling overboard rescue system is designed to help get the man overboard back onto *Ally Cat*— where they should have stayed in the first place.

Though it also serves as the "family car," our dinghy is an incredibly important piece of safety equipment. Just as there are trade-offs and compromises when buying a boat, the same applies to selecting equipment for the boat. We chose an inflatable, over a hard dinghy, primarily because we would be able to explore further and more efficiently. Inflatables are easy to get up on a plane, which allows us to move faster *on* the water rather than more slowly *through* it.

We went with the AB 9.5-foot aluminum Hypalon rigid inflatable boat (RIB). Our primary needs were for relatively lighter weight and the desire to stay dry-ish. We opted for a flat interior sole in the dinghy, which added to the overall weight, but made it much more user friendly. I am not the most coordinated person. Given that she weighed in at 106 pounds, Michael had to reinforce the davit mounts to hold her.

Originally, we had a little two-horsepower, two-stroke air-cooled engine for the dinghy—the one that washed ashore during Hurricane Sandy. We definitely wanted an engine with more horsepower; however, changes in emission laws in 2012 made small two-strokes a thing of the past in the United States. A four-stroke engine would be too heavy for me to maneuver. And maybe even for Michael, too. Plus, the weight was not ideal for *Ally Cat*. The Bahamas' emission laws, however, are a bit more lax. We bought our Yamaha 15-horsepower, two-stroke engine in Nassau just after we arrived in the Bahamas.

Given the pep and horsepower of her new engine, we finally settled on a name for the dinghy: *Rocket*. (I firmly believe *Rocket* is a he; Michael and Ally disagree). S/he was *so* easy to get up on a plane, and, man, she could fly! *Rocket* came outfitted with oars, as dinghy engines are notoriously fickle about starting. Additionally, we added an anchor and three of the orange Type II life jackets. And as I mentioned earlier, the portable VHF and a flashlight went in the dinghy every time she was deployed.

Over the course of the winter, Michael steadily checked items off of his boat projects lists. Meanwhile, my lists were growing and in need of my attention.

CHAPTER 10

MY LISTS HAVE LISTS

"Simplify, simplify, simplify." — *Henry David Thoreau*

In addition to the list of charts, guides, and other reference books (see Appendix A and B), Michael's lists of boat projects, things to buy, and tools and spare parts to bring (see Chapter 8: Boat Projects and Online Boyfriends), I had so many other lists multiplying in the months leading up to our departure it would have been helpful to have a Master List of all of my lists!

Okay, it wasn't quite that bad. However, I am glad started an Excel spreadsheet workbook very early in our planning process to capture all of my lists in one place. Simply called "The Plan," this workbook had the following tabs: Mail, Banking, and Legal; Rental Properties; First Aid, Prescriptions, and Toiletries; Galley; Packing List; Meadowbrook Lane; and Homeschool.

Mail, Banking, and Legal

We planned to sail for two years, though we also had a fallback plan of one year (ish) if things were not working out well. And I did not realize it was an option until we were in Grenada a year in, we even discussed adding a third year to explore the western Caribbean. Sigh.

I *really* wanted to explore the western Caribbean; however, another year on the boat was just not in our best interests as

141

a family. At the end of two years, Ally was twelve and ready to start junior high. As an only child, we really felt she needed to be with peers.

The idea of going through the Panama Canal on my very own boat made me giddy, as did the possibility of exploring the Galapagos and many islands of French Polynesia. However, the idea that once through the canal, it was two-plus weeks to the Galapagos and then three weeks or more to get to the Society Islands was still unappealing. Nope. Not for this crew.

At any rate, the move from our house was a temporary one. All along, we planned to return to Mattapoisett and move back into our house on Meadowbrook Lane. We opened a PO Box at our local post office to keep our world local. Once we had "moved" into the tiny eleven-inch by six-inch box—good practice for moving onto the 34-foot boat!—I set about the task of changing our address.

In 2007, as we planned our first RV trip, I aimed to reduce the amount of paper mail we received. The first step was cutting down on the volume of junk mail. At that time, I searched the internet and came up with a dozen strategies to reduce or eliminate unwanted mail, all of which I implemented. Over the years, junk mail gradually began to trickle in again, prompting me to repeat the process in 2013. The steps I took evolved over time. I searched "how can I reduce junk mail" on Google and selected Eco-Cycle's "How to Stop Junk Mail in Six Easy Steps." I followed their advice, which wasn't drastically different from what I had done eight years prior, just more streamlined and entirely online. Give it a try; it's an effective way to minimize the junk!

Any time I order anything online, I end up with a paper catalog in my mailbox within the month. Regularly, I pick up the phone and update my preferences to not receive a catalog via mail—with the exception of Fedco Seeds, High Mowing Organic Seeds, and Johnny Selected Seeds. Just about my favorite day all winter is the arrival of my seed catalogs.

I opted out of paper statements for bank and credit card accounts, as well as any utility bills for which this option was available. I pay all our bills online, preferring to centralize the process through Bank of America's online banking rather than dealing with each individual vendor. This practice significantly helps during tax season, too. If e-bills are available, I usually select that option, typically choosing to automatically pay the full amount one day before the due date. For credit cards, my approach has varied—sometimes, I opt to pay the minimum, and other times I pay the balance in full. My primary goal is to avoid any late fees. However, I also understand the argument that fraud might go unnoticed if one pays in full automatically. In my experience, the credit card companies' fraud departments have been more capable—or at least more sensitive—than I have in detecting fraud.

We carried an American Express card, as the "points" were deposited into Ally's 529 College Savings Plan with Fidelity. Not everyone accepts American Express, so we carried a Visa as a backup card. We decided to get a third card, just in case, and opened a MasterCard before leaving, as well.

I made sure to check all the expiration dates on all of our credit cards and ATM cards and *thought* we were good to go.

I did not count on the new chip technology debuting while we were in the Caribbean and the fact that the credit card companies automatically sent out new cards. We didn't even know to look for them! Oh well. And we also didn't plan on Fidelity ending their partnership with American Express, closing down our account, and automatically opening a new Visa for us. For the life of me, I couldn't figure that one out for a long time. Gratefully, our ATM cards continued to work until we were back in the States to pick up our new chip-enabled credit cards.

Once the amount of actual mail was reduced, I set about the relatively simple task of changing our address to our new PO Box. We made arrangements for the few bills we still received by mail to be paid and hoped nothing fell between the cracks. Amazingly, we incurred only two late fees in the entire two years, and when we came back to the States for a visit halfway through our trip, only one thing had fallen between the cracks. Okay, so it was kind of a big thing: our life insurance was canceled for nonpayment. I thought I had scheduled a recurring annual payment, but I had set up only a single payment. We were able to get Michael's reinstated while we were home in 2015; mine went back into effect the year we returned home. Good thing we did not die. The lesson I learned is that planning is great, and it served us well to plan in detail. However, it is nearly impossible to plan for every little thing. Just deal with the fallout as it reveals its ugly little self.

In terms of legal "stuff," we updated Ally's passport, though Michael and I were all set. We also made some changes to our wills. It seemed like a good idea to make sure all our affairs were in order prior to departure. Not that we planned to die, particularly since our life insurance was canceled. We created a limited power of attorney, which we granted to my girlfriend, Laurie. This gave her the ability to manage anything that had to do with our rental properties. She was only limited in that she couldn't sell them. We did find out later that she was not able to open or close escrow accounts as tenants turned over. It was a little annoying and slightly inconvenient, but not a showstopper.

Rental Properties

Speaking of Laurie, for each of our rental properties in Onset, I created a detailed information sheet. I included the tenants' contact and lease information, mortgage and tax payments and contact information, utility information, local contractors and contact information, and neighbor contact information. This consolidated a lot of information onto a few sheets of paper, which I was able to review with Laurie. It also made for a smooth transition when Laurie handed over the property management to Danielle.

We tried to take care of any outstanding items that needed to be repaired and ensure that all the properties were in good shape. My list also included letting our tenants know what we were up to and reassuring them that Laurie, and then Danielle, would be every bit as responsive to their needs as we had been.

First Aid, Prescriptions, and Toiletries

This list helped me build *Ally Cat's* first aid kit. A well-stocked kit can mean the difference between life and death. Though none of our planned passages exceeded three days, that can be a very long time if your body is fighting an infection. We worked with our primary-care physician and Ally's pediatrician to amass a variety of antibiotics to fight various infections, in both pediatric and adult doses, plus a few other medications our doctors suggested:

- Amoxicillin: This is a penicillin antibiotic used to treat chest and ear infections, particularly in children, as well as dental infections.

- Augmentin or Amoxicillin and Clavulanate (also known as Amox-Clav): This is a penicillin and beta-lactamase antibiotic used to treat bacterial infections in the ears, lungs, sinuses, skin, and urinary tract.

- Azithromycin (also known as Z-Pac): This macrolide antibiotic, i.e., non-penicillin antibiotic, is used to treat bacterial infections of the sinus, lungs, ears, and other organs.

- Cefdinir (also known as Omnicef): This broad-spectrum cephalosporin antibiotic is used for bacterial infections of the skin, ears, sinuses, throat, and tonsils and for those caused by bronchitis and pneumonia.

- Cephalexin: This is a cephalosporin antibiotic used to treat urinary tract infections, respiratory infections, and other bacterial infections.

- Ciprofloxacin (also known as Cipro): This fluoro-quinolone antibiotic is used to treat typhoid fever, infectious diarrhea, and infections of the skin, bone and joints, and abdomen.

- Clarithromycin: This macrolide antibiotic is used to treat bacterial infections of the ears, sinuses, skin, and throat, as well as bronchitis and pneumonia.

- Doxycycline: This tetracycline antibiotic is used to treat a wide variety of bacterial infections, including chest, dental, skin, and intestinal infections, as well as eye infections. It can also be used to prevent malaria and is the antibiotic of choice for Lyme disease.

- Gentamicin: This aminoglycoside antibiotic, in the form of a topical ointment, is used to treat bacterial infections of the skin and eye.

- Neomycin Polymyxin Hydrocortisone: This is a combination of an aminoglycoside antibiotic and a corticosteroid. These drops are used to treat ear infections.

Cruising is an exceptionally healthy lifestyle, and thankfully, we didn't have to use many of these medications. I only had one sinus infection the entire time, which I successfully treated with Amox-Clav. Interestingly, while we were in sweltering Grenada—where *Ally Cat* was anchored for over three months during hurricane season among dozens of other cruisers, including nearly thirty kids—impetigo, a highly contagious bacterial skin infection usually prevalent in nursery schools, spread rapidly. Surprisingly, it wasn't Ally who needed treatment but Michael! He successfully completed a course of Cephalexin, and we even shared our second adult prescription with another cruiser. It was reassuring to know we had everything we needed.

Cuts were a very real likelihood aboard or while exploring on shore. In addition to the standard fare of antimicrobial wash, hydrogen peroxide, triple antibiotic ointment, band-aids, and bandages, we carried gauze pads, wraps, tape, plus Steri-Strips for more serious cuts. Though Steri-Strips are not as strong as sutures, the thin adhesive strips can do the job even on stitch-worthy cuts. Some cruisers carry a suture kit, and I thought about it, but let's face it, it was not likely I was ever going to be able to sew someone up. Never say never, I suppose, but it was *highly* improbable. We also carried benzoin tincture, which, in addition to its antimicrobial properties, is a topical adhesive agent helping bandages stay put. Liquid Bandage, an all-in-one antiseptic treatment and waterproof bandage, is our go-to for more minor cuts and while the bigger ones are healing.

We added moleskin, ace bandages, and a couple of different-sized splints to our first aid kit, plus Advil, Tylenol, Aleve, and an emergency supply of oxycodone hydrochloride (also known as OxyContin), a prescription narcotic pain medication. We added Boiron Arnicare Gel, a topical homeo-pathic remedy we used for more minor bruises and muscle aches and pains, to our kit, too. You would be amazed at the number of unidentified boat bruises (UBBs).

We carried several EpiPens in the event of a severe allergic reaction and Benadryl for more minor reactions. We also had cough and cold remedies, as well as Ondansetron, a prescription tablet for nausea and vomiting, and Prochlorperazine, a prescription suppository also for nausea and vomiting. In addition, we stocked dried ginger, Pepto Bismol, Tums, and oral rehydration salts. For possible ear infections, we had rubbing alcohol and wax on hand to keep ears dry. We carried Nystatin and Triamcinolone, a prescription cream for fungal infections, along with prescription-strength hydrocortisone and aloe for insect stings, sunburn, and other minor skin irritations. We even kept some meat tenderizer to treat jellyfish stings, though I've since learned that white vinegar—our go-to cleaning solution on board—works just as effectively.

Rounding out our well-stocked first aid kit were gloves, tweezers, and scissors, plus a mylar emergency blanket bag, which reflects body heat to protect against shock, hypothermia, and the elements.

I have asthma, which I treat with prescription maintenance and emergency inhalers, and I take a couple of other prescriptions to treat depression. Michael has high cholesterol, which he treats with prescription medication. I find dealing with mail-order drug companies is horrific enough when I am at home with a reliable phone and internet, not to mention a stable mailing address. I really could not imagine trying to make it work while living on a boat.

Though everything else eventually worked out, the first year of managing prescription medications was every bit the nightmare I thought it might be. The issue with mail order was that although they shipped a ninety-day supply at a time, there was insufficient time for the medications to be shipped to Laurie and then forwarded to us, regardless of our location. Receiving mail in the Bahamas or practically anywhere else in the eastern Caribbean was nearly impossible without significant effort and time. I had thought Puerto Rico and the US Virgin Islands might be exceptions since they are US territories, but unfortunately, I was mistaken.

We barely made it through the first year and had to implement Plan B for the second year. During our visit home halfway through our trip, I filled all of our prescriptions at once, securing a twelve-month supply through Canada Drugs Online instead of using our mail-order pharmacy. This move cost us around $2,500 out-of-pocket, a significant portion of which we could have saved through our insurance. However, the peace of mind gained from knowing my maintenance asthma inhaler supply would not be interrupted was invaluable. After all, breathing isn't optional.

While I did not immediately get seasick on *Ally Cat* the minute I left the cockpit, as I had on our monohull, we really had very little experience sailing her. The trip included a lot of different types of sailing than we had ever done before, such as longer passages, night sailing, and open water sailing, and we wanted to be prepared. The most common seasickness remedy available over the counter in the United States is dimenhydrinate, also known as Dramamine, and meclizine, also known as Bonine. These tablets, if taken ahead of time, can help prevent seasickness or lessen the symptoms. They can also be taken as symptoms arise. Dramamine causes *significant* drowsiness, and Bonine somewhat less. There is also the prescription scopolamine patch, which is used to prevent—not treat—nausea and vomiting.

Ally appeared to be the most affected by seasickness in the beginning. Since she was not integral to running the boat day to day, it was all right if she was knocked out by Dramamine, so we brought a supply of it for her. Michael tried the scopolamine patch and vowed *never* again. It made him feel woozy. Not exactly prime condition to run a boat. And I felt terrific all the way to Washington, DC.

In DC, from other cruisers, we learned about cinnarizine, also known as Stugeron, which is widely used in Mexico and Europe and is available over the counter in most countries. Cinnarizine is an antihistamine with anti-sickness properties, which helps prevent *and* treat nausea and vomiting. Studies have shown that it is the most effective drug in treating motion sickness with the least amount of drowsiness. It is, however, not marketed in the United States or Canada due to its calcium channel-blocking properties, potentially causing drug-induced Parkinson's disease. Sigh. When we were able, we stocked up on Stugeron, and we took it prophylactically before long passages.

I kept a full list of the toiletries we used regularly. And while people brush their teeth everywhere, thereby ensuring we would be able to buy toothpaste just about anywhere we traveled, oftentimes we did not see familiar brands, and it was almost always more expensive than we were accustomed to. Small things like sunscreen or toothpaste, which we bought in bulk less expensively prior to departure, made sense to bring; things like toilet paper did not. As I was planning, I intended to bring some items with us, do a major shop in Florida before we left the States (and after I figured out storage on *Ally Cat*!), and then resupply many items in Puerto Rico, where we would be able to find stores such as Wal-Mart or Sam's Club. For us, this worked beautifully. However, the year after we came home, in 2017, was when hurricanes Irma and Maria tore through the eastern Caribbean. Given the damage sustained in Puerto Rico, we likely would have had to make a different provisioning plan.

Galley

I included all the pots and pans, utensils, and other galleyware we wanted on board in this list. Additionally, I listed the staples, spices, and nonperishables that we wanted to have aboard. This list made shopping easy and complete. Then, when I put things away on *Ally Cat*, I noted the quantity and location. Indeed, it would be a bad day if we ran out of coffee—and an even worse day if I knew we had some but couldn't find it. I rearranged my gallery numerous times in the first few months until I arrived at a livable setup, updating this master list, which proved invaluable.

As was the case aboard both *Mad Hatter* and *Wayward,* we opted not to put any electrical outlets in the galley in *Ally Cat.* We never had a microwave or toaster oven and did not feel the need for them on *Ally Cat* either. One of the best parts of sailing, for me, has always been "boat coffee." We use a French press on the boat. With no paper filter, the French press uses force to press the coffee to the bottom, and more of the oil is left to flavor the coffee. Best. Coffee. Ever. And no electric coffee pot.

For cooking and baking, our arsenal consisted of knives, wooden spoons, a whisk, a potato masher, and a grater, rather than a mixer or food processor. Ally learned how to bake on *Ally Cat*, so our rudimentary tools and making everything from scratch were all she knew. Her face was priceless the first time she used our KitchenAid mixer after we returned home!

The night before we left, friends dropped by with a couple of going-away presents: a nice bottle of rum for Michael and a copy of *The Boat Galley Cookbook: 800 Everyday Recipes and*

Essential Tips for Cooking Aboard by Carolyn Shearlock and Jan Irons. I had no idea how much I did not know about cooking aboard. Sure, I managed wonderful meals for a couple of weeks when we were on vacation, with well-stocked US grocery stores available before heading out and also while we were underway. How would I do when onions, carrots, cabbage, and potatoes were the only fresh produce available? I read that cookbook from the time we left Mattapoisett until we docked in Washington, DC. See Chapters 15: A Gardener Without a Garden and 16: We're Cruising to witness my metamorphosis into galley goddess!

Packing List

This list was perfect for capturing anything that did not fit under the First Aid, Prescriptions, and Toiletries or Galley lists. It was also a great placeholder for items we wanted to buy before the trip and a way to remember what research we did and where we decided to buy it. I also used this list to keep track of books I wanted to load onto our Kindles.

Meadowbrook Lane

To make the money work for us, we had to cover our expenses on our land-based home while we were away. In addition to packing what we needed to move on to *Ally Cat*, we packed up and moved all our personal belongings out of our house. We rented our home furnished, thank goodness, and we were able to store our personal belongings in the attic, both eves, a huge walk-in closet (formerly the "boat closet") and even in Michael's office downstairs, eliminating the need for costly storage space.

There was *a lot* of purging going on in the months leading up to our departure. I'm pretty sure both Michael and Ally were a little worried *they* might be put out front for one of the charity shops to pick up. This list covered each area of the house I needed to purge and pack up, in addition to the house projects to be completed before renting it out. It was quite satisfying to check each item off, one by one. Why did we put off many of these projects until someone else was going to be living in our home? I suppose I have always heard the saying that a house never looks better than when it goes on the market. Once we had a signed lease and a deposit, first and last month's rent, we were committed to moving aboard *Ally Cat* for at least a year.

Homeschool

Though the Homeschool tab was empty for an unnervingly long time, it was a great placeholder for the books, websites, blogs, etc., that people invariably recommended when they found out what we were up to. And as I gradually learned more and more, I used this space to capture more and more information. This list didn't go away once we headed out in *Ally Cat*. In fact, I started an entire workbook entirely for homeschooling, with a tab for each subject. I captured what Ally did as we went along, resulting in an end-of-year portfolio for her school back home with very little effort. Along with its own workbook in Excel, homeschooling was so big, it deserved its own chapter. Please read on for much more information about our boatschool experience in the next chapter. And yes, I had to add the word "boatschool" to the dictionary on my laptop.

CHAPTER 11

BOATSCHOOLING

"And then I realized adventures are the best way to learn." — Anonymous

As we created our lists of projects to complete, items to buy and things to do before departure, steadily checking them off one by one, the innocuous-looking item "Homeschool" continued to linger, untouched. During those days, not to mention the ensuing two years of travel, I pushed myself outside my comfort zone in so many ways, but the idea of taking on the responsibility of educating our daughter seemed to be the most daunting. Questions about school came up every time I told someone about our trip. They would ask, "What curriculum are you planning to use?"

"Can I really do this?" I asked myself regularly. Egad. At that point, I was not even sure what the word "curriculum" actually meant!

The answer was yes, though I was only able to say that with confidence once we were back home, and Ally confidently navigated seventh grade in our public school system.

After working around it for months, because the idea of homeschooling terrified me, I finally set aside a full week to tackle it. I was determined to sort out what materials we would need and check "Homeschool" off my list. I called the school superintendent's office to determine the mechanics of withdrawing Ally, what was needed from us to homeschool for the two years, and what would be needed to re-register her when we returned. In response to my call, via email, I received an eight-page Home Education Policy to review.

The three-page description, including a review of Massachusetts General Laws Chapter 76, Sections 1, 2, and 4, which provide the legal basis for what we were doing, gave me a succinct overview. The two-page Notice of Intent to Pursue a Program of Home Education had to be submitted annually for the superintendent's approval.

Again, that nagging question, "Am I really qualified to teach Ally for two years?"

I did take a small measure of comfort in the thought I couldn't completely ruin her academically in two years. Right? Michael and I talked about this at length. We firmly believed the life experiences during our two-year adventure far outweighed the risk that Ally might lose some ground academically. We reasoned that if she was behind in any areas when we returned to our public schools for junior high, we would simply work with her teachers and utilize tutors, if necessary. And Ally was firmly on board with this idea. Though Michael and I were comfortable making the decisions together for our family, we also fully understood the importance of having Ally's buy-in. This boatschooling experiment was definitely going to be a participatory sport for all!

The final section asked us what method of assessment we would use and to provide a description. It also noted that we were expected to share these assessments annually with the principal. Our options were:

1. Daily logs, journals, progress reports, portfolios, or dated work samples.

2. An independent report made by someone acceptable to both the superintendent and the parents.

3. Standardized test results.

4. Consultation with the superintendent or principal.

5. Any other method agreed to by both the superintendent and parents.

By signing and submitting this form, along with the appropriate attachments, I also agreed to provide a minimum of 900 hours of instruction for Ally as an elementary-age child (the requirement was 990 hours for secondary-age children).

I definitely had more research to do before I could complete that form.

I set up a meeting with Ally's principal. Though we had just learned he would be leaving our district in a few weeks, he had been at her school for a number of years and still could provide valuable information. During our meeting, he gave me a copy of the 2011 Massachusetts Frameworks for Math and English Language Arts (ELA) and suggested I spend some time on the Massachusetts Department of Elementary and Secondary Education (DESE) website to become familiar with the resources available. He also gave me some sage advice: keep her writing, study revolutions and civil wars—not just ours, but throughout the world—and make sure she is comfortable with technology, Google Docs, and online assessments. He looked around his office, searching for materials he could pass along to me. In addition to the frameworks, he also gave me a fifth-grade math textbook, and a well-loved copy of *Where the Red Fern Grows*, by Wilson Rawls, required summer reading for incoming sixth-graders.

"Okay, what did I plan on teaching Ally? What *should* my child be learning in fifth and sixth grades?" I thought that was a straightforward question. I was wrong. If you think there is no definitive manual on how to raise your child, try to find one to help you homeschool. It was not that there were no books or websites; it was that there were way too many with conflicting and confusing information.

"I am a reasonably intelligent person," I reminded myself. "Surely I can come up with what Ally needs to learn for fifth and sixth grades."

Apparently, my notion of a checklist of skills and information for my child to learn in a given year was not an idea to which DESE subscribed. Though I had a hard copy of the Frameworks, also known as standards, which were also posted on the DESE website for English Language Arts and Math, these Common Core Standards, developed in 2009-10, were what students should know and be able to do. Curriculum is how students will learn it, to be determined by local districts or, in our case, by me. How could I possibly come up with the tools to teach her if I did not know what information she needed to learn?

Though not exactly what I was hoping for, the DESE Frameworks were a start. For ELA and math, at least. What about science, history, and geography, not to mention art, computers and technology, music, physical education, and foreign language? I definitely had my work cut out for me.

That was the exact state of mind I was in when I arrived at a restaurant to meet my friend Andrea for lunch. I needed to vent, so I asked her if she understood how convoluted the available information on homeschooling was.

"Yes," she said. "Yes, in fact, I do."

She shared what she called her "dirty little secret"— not only did her four boys attend public school, but she homeschooled them on the side. What?! Across from me sat a dear friend from my early mom days; she has a PhD in mathematics, and her husband is a neurosurgeon. I had the utmost respect for these two when it came to educating their children. "You homeschool? Do tell, please!"

We set up a time later that week for her to do a little show-and-tell for me to see what materials she used and to get the CliffsNotes version of what she learned over the years. When I arrived at her house later that week, she had a stack of books on her kitchen table. Pen and notebook at the ready, I sat down next to her. She started with *The Core Knowledge Sequence for Preschool–Grade 8: Content and Skill Guidelines for Grades K-8*. What do you know? A list, by grade, of what my child should be learning.

First, there was a concise overview of topics, basically an outline and details, listed by subject, not only for math and language arts but for science, history and geography, visual arts, and music, as well. I felt as if I had struck gold! Amazingly, this information is available online to download at no cost, though I did decide I wanted a hard copy of the book, which I purchased.

Andrea then went on to tell me about the companion series, *What Your (First to Sixth) Grader Needs to Know* books, edited by E. D. Hirsch Jr., founder of the Core Knowledge Foundation, an independent nonprofit educational organization. I immediately ordered the fourth-grade book, finding a great used copy on Amazon, to compare it to what Ally was learning at that time. These books are available in Kindle format as well, though I found used paperback versions for both fifth and sixth grades, too.

I loved that this gave me both a broad sense of what Ally should be learning as well as details. I still needed to determine the *curriculum* we would use, though I had a much better idea of what I wanted it to cover. We also used these books to review at the end of the year and to provide a smoother transition after a break in schooling.

In addition to this treasure trove, Andrea also shared what curricula they had used and what worked well for her boys, as well as what didn't. Though this was valuable, every child has a different learning style, so I still needed to figure out a lot of this on my own. However, I had my checklist! Score.

I asked how she assessed her kids and determined progress was being made. Though she definitely felt it had limitations, she used standardized tests, and she pointed me in the direction of Seton Testing Services. For less than $30, I was able to order the California Achievement Test (CAT) and administer it to my daughter at my convenience. Once I sent her answer sheet and testing materials back, within two or three days, I could see Ally's results online, and I received a hard copy within a week by mail. I ordered the fourth-grade test at the end of the school year. Not surprisingly, she did very well. Midsummer before we left, I ordered the fifth-grade test. Again, she did very well, but more importantly, this provided a benchmark to measure her progress the following year.

All that was left to check this item off my list was to determine the curriculum. I finally understood what it meant, although that word is often used in multiple contexts and can be confusing. By curriculum, I meant I needed to determine what materials—or books—we were going to use.

About the time I was seriously mulling this over, I ran into my neighbor, a retired teacher who taught fifth through eighth grades in local public schools for more than twenty years. Since homeschooling was on my brain, we talked a bit about our plans. He said he had a shelf full of materials that I was welcome to have. I thanked him and said I would stop by to pick them up.

"No problem. I will bring them to your house later today," he said. And he did. He showed up with a wheelbarrow and four boxes of materials! We were going to need a bigger boat.

I put the boxes in the middle of our family room, which forced me to go through them immediately. Again overwhelmed, the only thing I could do was to separate them by subject matter: math, ELA, science, history, and geography. I was pretty sure I had enough material to teach Ally for the next ten years. I clearly did not have the skills to determine which, among this plethora of teaching materials, was worthy of using, so I shelved them in Ally's playroom until I figured something out.

There they sat for a month or more. Already out of my comfort zone, I called Monica, a mom I barely knew. Her daughter was Ally's age and had once come to Ally's birthday party several years before. Monica was a sixth-grade science teacher in a neighboring town, and her husband, also a science teacher, had just been named as the new principal at Ally's school. Monica and I share a passion for gardening, so I invited her over to see my gardens and would she possibly be able to help me sort through all of my books. She not only agreed, but she was delighted to help. Over the years, she had sat on many curriculum review and selection committees and brought that invaluable experience.

At that time, I was also trying to figure out storage bins to fit into each of our unique-sized locker storage areas. One thing about a boat, it does not stay dry all the time. That, coupled with insane humidity and salt air, made it necessary to store items in Ziplock bags in watertight bins. If you care about what is inside, that is. I had just discovered a space and bins that I thought would be perfect for our school materials. The space on the port side, under the navigation station, between our chart locker and safety locker, accommodated eight scrapbook bins that I discovered on clearance at the craft store. Using masking tape and a Sharpie, I labeled each one: math, science, ELA, social studies, geography, Spanish, and art. The final bin was for Ally's pencils, pens, and other school supplies.

Monica was amazing and exactly what I needed when I needed her! She was able to go through each piece of material and quickly assess if it was good, meh, dated, better for fifth or sixth grade, or not appropriate at all. Soon we had a pile for each subject for each year and a pile to donate to the library. Would you believe that every item she selected for fifth grade for each subject fit exactly into its designated bin for that subject? It was astounding. And I had sixth grade planned out, too.

Just so you don't think that life was too easy, school did not always go according to plan. First, there was the fact that Ally was a kid, and I was her mom. We had to figure out our new roles as teacher and student. While I was all-fired ready to teach her, at first, she stubbornly (wonder where she gets that?) refused to learn from me. I had to get rid of the idealized notion of what I thought boatschool should look like and accept where we were. What that meant for me was to embrace the tremendous nontraditional classroom we had available—all of Washington, DC, and down the East Coast—and to figure out how to make our learning fun.

Finding the right math curriculum also took some doing. I started with the textbook Ally's principal gave us. Ally informed me she didn't like working out of a textbook; she preferred worksheets. Ever resourceful, I took the X-Acto knife and cut out the pages for each day. Voila! Worksheets. Not surprisingly, she still was not crazy about it, though somehow, I think that was more about her mom outsmarting her than anything else. In the end, we both agreed the old textbook was not the right fit for us.

Since I did not have a teacher's manual to go along with the textbook, I had to work out each problem in order to correct her work. Though I am solid in fifth-grade math, that one subject took a lot of my time, unnecessarily. After looking around, we decided to try Singapore Math. Thank goodness for Amazon, as we had our new workbook in two days, complete with an answer key.

This worked well until, well until it didn't. We came across a concept that was not explained in a way that Ally easily understood. I tried to explain it, Mrs. Mom style. No dice. We went back to the original textbook, and though it worked for that particular concept, it wasn't until April 2015, almost three-quarters of the way through fifth grade, that we were introduced to Teaching Textbooks, an award-winning math app, when we were in St. Martin.

At last, we found the solution we had been looking for.

Ally took the placement test online (gratefully, we had decent internet access), and a fellow cruiser loaned me the CD for Math 6. Ally loved it! My friend Kim was flying in to visit a few days later, so once again, Amazon to the rescue. I shipped the CDs and workbook, along with some boat parts, to Kim, and she schlepped it all to St. Martin.

Though we didn't start the Teaching Textbooks Math 6 until the end of April, Ally did manage to get through both Math 6 and Math 7 by the following June. She loved it, and math took absolutely *no* preparation time from me. Definitely a win-win. And, I have to brag, she tested into advanced math for seventh grade, which helped allay my fears that I had ruined her academically. Do yourself a favor; if you ever need to teach a child math, check out Teaching Textbooks first.

Though I am a writer, I struggled to get Ally to write, even as the principal's words, "Keep her writing," echoed ad nauseam in my ears. I think my standards were (and still are) too high; I have the notion that she should be able to write somewhere around a college level, never mind that she was in fifth grade when we started. A definite shortcoming on my part and one I somewhat successfully navigated. I tried to back away from critique and instead focus on some tools to help her become a better writer, such as researching topics and creating a solid outline before starting to write.

I also prayed that along the way, she would encounter a teacher, you know, that really special teacher, who would ignite a passion for writing. Amazingly, that happened our first year back. Her English teacher, Mr. Orie, asked her if she would be willing to do a yearlong writing project. She was still responsible for the same types of writing as her class-mates, only she would have an alternate prompt and would create her memoir of our trip by the end of the year. She came downstairs one morning early in the school year and said, "I am *so* excited to write about our trip!" Wow. Who is this child, and what have you done with my daughter?

Here are a couple of additional thoughts on boatschooling. We met lots of kids along the way, and what was clear was that decisions about how to teach your own child are about as individual as each child. There are so many ways to homeschool; don't get discouraged if your first attempt is not a resounding success. We pieced together Ally's curriculum since we were given a pile of terrific resources, and we assumed we would not have internet. As it turned out, that was a good call since it was hit or miss the entire trip. We just as easily could have chosen one of the complete grade-level curriculums, such as Calvert with their ginormous stack of books and matching price, or the free online all-in-one Easy Peasy, or even one of the online virtual schools. There are lots of choices.

Two weeks after we left Massachusetts, after our *vacation*, Ally and I officially started the first day of fifth grade with the help of the incomparable interactive classroom of Washington, DC. To say we saw and learned a lot in our nation's capital is an understatement. In seven weeks, we went on thirty bona fide field trips, including visits to nearly all of the Smithsonian museums, galleries, and zoo; more than a dozen monuments and memorials; Arlington National Cemetery, the Washington National Cathedral, and Mount Vernon. With some homeschooling creativity, we added at least ten more outings that could be counted as field trips, such as a Washington Nationals baseball game and the Annapolis Boat Show.

We went on so many field trips I struggled with the best way to reinforce what we learned before moving on to the next experience. It was particularly difficult as we often learned events out of chronological order. For example, on our first day in DC, we went to the Thomas Jefferson Memorial and then to the Washington Monument, honoring our third president (1801-1809) and our first president (1789-1797), respectively. In an effort to create some sense of time for the important events we were learning about, we opted for a very low-tech option: index cards and a plastic expandable coupon file. After a day of exploration, we would talk about what we saw and learned that day.

For example, when we went to the Washington Monument, we talked about George Washington, a senior officer in the French and Indian War, the commander-in-chief of the Continental Army during the Revolutionary War, a Founding Father of the United States, one of the authors of the Constitution and the first president of the United States. That one monument would generate a number of index cards—one for each important event or person. On the front, Ally wrote the event or person and the date associated with it; on the back, she wrote a few sentences about the person or event. In this manner, we were able to talk about our field trips, make note of key people and events, and finally put much of our nation's history into a chronological timeline.

In Appendix C, I included the letters I attached to our Notice of Intent to Pursue a Program of Home Education for both fifth and sixth grades in the event they are helpful. Remember: make plans, don't plan the outcome

I found I had much more in the way of teaching materials than was necessary. However, I almost always had what I needed, and therefore, I don't regret having too much. And in true cruiser fashion, I passed along just about everything to other kids' boats before we left the Bahamas. Some of the history-related materials I have kept, having discovered how much I love historical fiction.

Finally, I was *thrilled* to find the Facebook group, Homeschooling Around the World. I cannot say enough great things about this group. Lots of knowledge, lots of links to free resources, and lots of committed parents taking responsibility for their kids' education. Do yourself a favor and join. I loaded our Kindles with free and low-cost books based on information I learned from this group. Months into our trip, when I was planning a unit on volcanoes (we visited about a dozen volcanic islands and almost as many volcanoes), I searched on my Kindle and came up with eight books, all downloaded for free, to use during that unit study. Likewise, when Ally was obsessed with Greek and Roman mythology, I had dozens of books to read with her. Though I didn't find it until quite late in our trip, BookBub and Early Bird Books were fabulous resources for free and inexpensive books, too.

It was a positive experience on the whole; however, I have to admit I was *thrilled* to retire from boatschooling once we returned home.

CHAPTER 12

THE GIFT OF YOGA

"The secret of change is to focus all of your energy not on fighting the old, but on building the new." —Socrates

D are I admit that life at home was somewhat out of control the week before we tossed the dock lines? Let's be honest. It was utter chaos. There was, however, one perfectly calm hour in our house that week.

I started practicing yoga more than thirty years ago. As a runner, I was used to a rigid training schedule as I constantly increased my distances from a few miles to full marathons. Yoga was very different for me, an enigma of sorts. It provides a foundation to continually strive to improve without the need to perpetually "up my game." And I really believe it makes me a better person. It also reminds me that unless I take the time to care for myself physically, mentally, emotionally, and spiritually, I am unable to care for others in my life.

For the first five or six years I practiced, I took the occasional live class, usually while on vacation or when I happened upon one that was convenient for me with my crazy travel schedule. As a consultant for Oracle, I traveled Monday through Thursday every week, so I took my yoga practice with me, first on a VHS tape (don't laugh, I'm old), then on DVD, to practice in my hotel room. When I was pregnant with Ally and stopped traveling, I signed up for a prenatal class at The Yoga Studio in our town. After Ally was born, and I struggled to redefine myself as a stay-at-home mom, I started a regular Tuesday morning yoga class with Donna, the owner of The Yoga Studio.

Michael still traveled every week on the same Monday-through-Thursday schedule I had kept, and I was home alone with Ally all week. When Michael and I were engaged in 2002, I sold my house in Nashville and moved to Massachusetts, knowing virtually no one other than Michael. I always had a tremendous support system in my girlfriends, both near and far, but for the first time, I had no local friends. People said I would meet lots of new people once we had kids. So when Ally was born, I wondered when the new friends would come.

"Oh, it'll come. You know, when she starts school and gets into activities," they said. Oh, dear. I would be taken away in a not-so-flattering little white suit to a rubber-lined room by then.

I did manage to build a tremendous village locally, but it took time. Michael and I, along with his sister Beth, and our nieces, joined the church where we visited for much of a year when Ally was eleven days old. Slowly, over time, we became part of a church family. When a neighbor, with whom I was friendly in passing, and I emerged from our heavy winter coats in the spring of 2004, it was clear we were both very pregnant. Our girls were born a month apart. When Ally was three months old, she asked if I would like to try a Music Together class with her in town.

"Yes!!" Too eager?

At music class a few months later, one of the other moms who had a son Ally's age asked if I might be interested in going to a playgroup with her at a church in the next town. Again, I probably sounded a bit too enthusiastic, but it was worth it as my love affair with the Fairhaven MOMS (Moms Offering Moms Support) Club began. From small playgroups in each other's homes and library story times to blueberry-picking excursions, camping, and service projects within our community, the MOMS Club was my primary social life and support system for the next five years. Even now, many of my closest friends—and Ally's, too!—are from those days. In fact, just the other night, more than a decade later, at a much-needed girls' night, Laurie, Marianne, and I, also known as the "Seed Sisters," raised a toast to the MOMS Club for providing such great friends and sanity. A lifeline, then and now.

Tuesdays became sacred. From 8:30 in the morning until 4:30 in the afternoon, the only responsibility I had was *me*. The same sweet gal who provided after-school care for my nieces many years ago, came in time for me to get to yoga class and stayed with Ally all day. In class, as we set an intention for our practice, mine was generally, "I am here. I am taking care of myself. I will continue to take care of myself. I am here."

Once nourished, physically and spiritually, I would spend the rest of the day any way I wanted or needed—running errands, going to the doctor, volunteering, or getting my hair cut. Sometimes, I stayed home, using the time to work in the garden or my home office, as I still kept the books for Michael's consulting company and managed our rental properties. This arrangement went on until Ally started kindergarten and was in school all day. By then, Miss Irene had become like a grandma to Ally and a cherished mother-in-law to me.

Over the years, I added a Saturday yoga class , as well. A second class was not only beneficial for me, but it also turned Saturday mornings into a special Daddy-Ally time. However, as we determined the budget for our upcoming trip, which required me returning to work, I regretfully had to give up my Tuesday class. Thankfully, I still had Saturdays! By then, Donna had closed The Yoga Studio, and one of her former teachers had opened a new studio in town where Donna taught her classes. As a devoted student, I followed, and so did many others.

One day, the winter before we left, Donna announced she would not be teaching Saturday classes for the spring session. She found a new teacher, Jody, to take over her class. I was devastated. One thing I discovered over the years is that all yoga instructors are not created equally.

I'll admit it. I do not like change. In fact, I rather abhor it. I know, I know. You are probably asking why I was planning to go live on a sailboat for two years—a lifestyle that is *all* about flexibility and going with the flow—if I couldn't even deal with a new yoga instructor for my Saturday morning class. Believe me, I asked myself the same thing. And I had a little chat with myself.

"Self, get over it. You need your Saturday morning yoga. Especially now. Go with an open mind. Go."

After all, I was every bit as resistant to the new yoga studio when we moved, and I grew to love that space over time. And so I went to Jody's class the following Saturday morning with an open mind. Guess what? I loved her. Donna had been her mentor; therefore, there were some much-appreciated similarities in their styles. Plus, Jody had this great trick of taking us through planks on our way to or from just about any pose. I was starting to love my newfound core strength, which was a plus for my balance, and a handy skill on a boat.

Yet another skill I clearly needed to hone, not only for our trip but for life in general, was learning to embrace change— maybe even to welcome it. From Greek philosophers to American authors, we've been told time and time again that the only constant is change. I might as well become friends with it. After all, change is neither good nor bad; it simply is. It has taken a lot of work on my part, and I'm not always successful, but I've found that approaching situations with an open mind, free from expectations and preconceived negativity, has become more the norm than the exception for me. Rather than rejecting or fearing change, I continue to work on my resilience when confronted with it.

With less than six weeks until we headed out in *Ally Cat*, stress levels were high, and my yoga practice was more important than ever. I had about five classes left on my class card and planned to use every last one. Unfortunately, Jody's schedule did not allow her to teach on Saturdays through the summer. When the spring session ended at the end of June, so would her class.

Jody, knowing I had classes left with her, offered to refund them. Taking an initial stab at bartering—yet another skill that would come in handy in our travels—I asked if she would let me tape a class at the studio and/or come to our house for a private session and let me tape it. She said, "Sure!" to both.

Thus, the one perfectly calm hour in our house four days before departure.

Michael took Ally and her best friend out for dinner and ice cream. (Tough duty, yet, being the great guy that he is, he's almost always willing to take one for the team!) Jody and I laid out our mats in my sunroom, my favorite room in the house. The music was perfect, neither too loud nor too low. Jody's voice was soothing and easy to hear. Listening to the symphony of "summer bugs" just beyond the screened-in porch during relaxation pose couldn't have been more fitting. Of course, just to keep it real, the smoke detectors let out a crazy series of beeps about fifteen minutes in and again toward the end of our session. This was, of course, recorded right along with my beautiful yoga class.

From the moment I went up on the front deck of *Ally Cat* when we first saw the boat in Annapolis, I deemed it my yoga studio. It's a perfect wide-open space for my practice. And it's even big enough for two. I enjoyed my first "class" with Jody, courtesy of the video on my iPod (yep, old school again), while we were anchored in Atlantic Highlands, New Jersey, with smoke alarms and all. Talk about yoga with a serious view! I practiced while looking out over the anchorage and New York Harbor, right at the Manhattan skyline. Yoga is very different on a moving boat, requiring more balance than on land, creating much more of a core workout. Good thing Jody had taken us through planks all spring long.

Yoga continued to be a source of pleasure, exercise, meditation, and stress relief for me throughout our trip. I practiced with Jody via my iPod at least once a week for two years. I'd say I more than got my money's worth from my class card. In addition to the more than one hundred solo classes with Jody on the bow of *Ally Cat*, I had dozens of other opportunities to practice yoga. From a studio in a strip mall in Virginia to the beaches in the Bahamas and Bequia, from the lawn under an enormous tent set up for Holy Week in the Dominican Republic to the pavilion of a posh resort in St. Lucia, a portico among the Stations of the Cross in Martinique, and three different marinas in southern Grenada, each practice has its own memories.

Yoga on the beach is an opportunity to fully embrace your love of sand. Or not. Good thing we were always just mere steps from appealing turquoise water to rinse off. In my beloved Bequia, we ended relaxation with a tropical downpour—a freshwater rinse, also known as "liquid sunshine."

For my birthday, Michael and Ally gave me a day pass to True Blue Bay, an eco-friendly resort and marina in Grenada. I had no idea what a treat I was in for! Breakfast and lunch, yoga, and two swimming pools were mine for the day. The restaurant, The Dodgy Dock, is nestled among lush gardens, built on docks over the water. The yoga studio, Sankalpa, sitting on the second floor among the treetops, is virtually a big kids' tree house. Three "walls" of the studio were open floor-to-ceiling windows; the fourth was nonexistent, providing an unencumbered view of the bay.

Though the cruising community is as diverse as the ports from which they hail, I never had any trouble locating cruisers to join my yoga practice, some of whom were even instructors. I still believe not all yoga instructors are created equally; however, I now understand that each has something unique to offer. I also learned that no matter where I am, as soon as I step on my mat, I am once again in a familiar place. I am here.

Not long after we returned home in August 2016, I started Saturday morning yoga class again. And again, Donna was my instructor at the new location of her Yoga Studio. That winter, I returned to Donna's Tuesday class as well and to many of my old friends. Funny, after so much time and so many miles and locations, it seemed I had come full circle.

CHAPTER 13

ARE YOU READY?

If you surrender to the wind, you can ride it. — Toni Morrison

In the months leading up to our departure, I felt increasingly as if I was leading a double life: professional by day, mission-oriented trip planner by night and weekend. Not to mention Ally was still only nine, so homework helper, cook, chauffeur, laundry genie, and mom, as well. My inexpensive iced coffee fueled me just about every afternoon on my way home from work. Wonder Woman had nothing on me.

At work, my boss was fully aware of our plans before she hired me; however, very few others knew anything about my secret life. Though I enjoyed my coworkers and had become friendly with many, our plans were so far out of the norm for it was virtually impossible for others to relate. So we marched ahead with our to-do lists without much ado. Or much sleep.

Michael, on the other hand, had understandably kept our plans tightly under wraps at work. As a consultant, there are even fewer guarantees, in terms of continued employment, than as an employee. Without his income, there simply would not have been any trip. Therefore, no one from his project knew anything: the stops in Annapolis to look at boats, buying *Ally Cat*, our road trip to Annapolis to load and prep *Ally Cat*, the vacation to bring *Ally Cat* home to Massachusetts, packing up, and moving onto the boat, or renting out our house.

Nothing. Before we left Massachusetts, Michael gave notice to the company he was subcontracted through, providing an eleven-week notice. They decided not to inform the client until about four weeks out. The timing of his departure, set for early November, would not impact the project; however, disclosing it too soon could cause unwanted distractions.

So no one in Jacksonville knew anything about our plans or the miles-long list of boat projects. In the twelve months leading up to our departure, Michael was busier at work than I have ever seen him, in addition to his multitude of boat projects. He truly had become a world-class double agent.

During this time, well-meaning friends would ask him about boat projects. Clearly, Michael's least favorite question became, "Is the boat ready?" Um, no.

Though, it's important to point out that *no* boat will ever be *all* ready. Ask anyone who owns a boat if they are ever *done* with their list. Trust me, they will laugh. And as Michael says, "If you are going to cruise, you need to pick a date and go." He is good at prioritizing projects. Obviously, items affecting safety and a number of other projects had to be completed before we left. However, a good many other items on his list, say shelving for my pantry, could be pushed down the road. We had close to two months in Washington, DC, until he was finished with work, to whittle away at the list, where we were at a dock with good shopping and could easily order supplies, too. Besides, as I have heard many times, cruising is simply fixing your boat in exotic locations.

For me, by far, the most terrifying question I was asked for a long time was, "Oh, you will be homeschooling. What curriculum are you planning to use?" You saw how I finally overcame that fear in Chapter 11: Boatschooling. However, as time passed, and we were within six months of leaving, my new least favorite questions became, "Are you ready?" If they only knew.

We were steadily making progress on boat projects and the rest of our lists; however, the boat was an absolute wreck! *Ally Cat* was definitely way more workshop than home at this stage. I could barely walk around inside, let alone picture living there for two years. The cushions for our beds were still inside the house, upstairs in the hallway. The salon seats were covered in tools and project supplies. The galley—my kitchen!—was a full-on electrical shop, and the navigation station had more plumbing supplies than charts or guidebooks. No, we were definitely not ready!

We did, however, pick a departure date: August 23, 2014. We planned our trip for more than two years, aiming for that departure date. While we made progress toward our goal week by week, the two months before we left bordered on manic. With a lot of hard work, and some well-timed and well-appreciated help from family and friends, we were finally so close to being ready to go that we could almost taste it—the salt water, that is.

On August 22, the day before our scheduled departure date, I said, "We will sleep on the boat tomorrow night, even if it kills me."

Later in the day, however, I had an epiphany: deadlines, schedules, and rigid plans were not at all what we were trying to create with our out-of-the-norm travels. In fact, we were working toward just the opposite. This sabbatical was about adventure and peace and flexibility and self-sufficiency, and making smart decisions based on the weather, the circumstances, and our crew.

We pushed back our departure by two days.

I am so grateful for my sweet, very rational husband. And for starting the journey in a more reasonable frame of mind! On August 23, after waking to a magnificent sunrise over our cove, instead of "killing myself," I spent a beautiful afternoon in my gardens. It was the perfect way to say "so long" to my sanctuary. It was also the perfect reminder about the importance of deadlines—actually, the lack of deadlines.

Getting out of the house was brutal: last boxes to the attic, last bins to the donate pile, last bags to the trash, and last load for *Ally Cat* to the car.

Whew.

On August 25, 2014, Michael's fifty-fifth birthday, we drove to Leisure Shores Marina, just down the street from our house, where *Ally Cat* had been tied up for a week to load. Greeted by our own farewell crew, we loaded the last of our belongings into the dock cart and headed to *Ally Cat*.

Michael tried to warn me. All of those trips he and Ally had been making back and forth to the boat loading all of the stuff I packed and set out to go were on board. And they *filled* the salon. Oh my. Where to start? Apparently, the packing and sorting were not quite done. Kind of in a state of shock, we said our goodbyes and sailed out of the marina.

As we sailed out of our cove, our home behind us and the complete unknown ahead, I couldn't help thinking that I was leaving everything I knew and loved—with the exception of Michael and Ally. Talk about being pushed past my comfort zone in just about every direction. However, inside I was calm, at peace, and ready to begin our new life.

Or maybe I was just exhausted.

I unpacked and stored all the way to Cuttyhunk, the outermost of the Elizabeth Islands in Massachusetts, less than twenty miles from our cove. Amazingly, I cleared the salon enough to sit at the table for a lovely dinner of typical boat fare: grilled chicken, potatoes and onions, and cukes and tomatoes from the garden. We made a toast to our Crew of Three and Michael's birthday. We *were* ready!

Pirates

While questions about the readiness of the boat and crew were the most anxiety-inducing, we were asked some other questions frequently. Particularly common, though interestingly posed much more often to Michael than to me, were questions about pirates. Where we traveled, there was very little risk we would encounter pirates. Never say never, but the Bahamas, the Windward Passage, and the eastern Caribbean are just not hotbeds of that type of activity.

There is a resource within the cruising community called Noonsite. For more than twenty years, it has been a go-to website for cruisers, providing a multitude of information country by country, particularly when it comes to safety and security. Some islands or specific towns are fairly well known for more crime than others. For example, via Noonsite and fellow cruisers, we were warned about

Nassau in the Bahamas, Samanà in the Dominican Republic, Soufriere in St. Lucia, the island of St. Vincent, and both Canouan and Union Islands in the Grenadines. Though we made plans with current events in mind, we visited four of those six places with no incidents. And it is a reasonable argument that two of the most dangerous places we stopped throughout the whole trip were Washington, DC, and Miami, Florida.

Firearms

Another question we were asked frequently was, "Are you taking a gun?"

The simple answer was "No." We have never owned or used guns. We had no plans to purchase one and learn how to use it for the trip.

In case you are curious, firearms pose a tricky issue with Customs and Immigration. We checked in and out of sixteen different countries, in addition to the United States. While each country had slightly different regulations regarding firearms, they all required us to declare if we had any on board. In some countries, such as Turks and Caicos, you are required to surrender all firearms when you check in, to be returned upon check out.

Sometimes, as in Turks and Caicos, we did not check in and out of the same city or town. We checked in to Providenciales ("Provo") and checked out of South Caicos, about fifty miles away. As it was, after we checked out, we moved from South Caicos to Big Sand Cay, a little over twenty-five miles south, in order to stage ourselves to arrive in good light in Luperon,

Dominican Republic, more than ninety miles away. Though it would not be impossible, it would have added another level of complexity to our passage planning if we had to go back to Provo to check out and retrieve a firearm.

Though we did not visit every island in the Eastern Caribbean, we also found this surrender policy in the Dominican Republic, the British Virgin Islands, and St. Lucia. In Antigua and Barbuda, St. Kitts and Nevis, St. Lucia, St. Vincent and the Grenadines, and Grenada, you may be permitted to keep firearms on board in a sealed locker if Customs are satisfied that your boat has a "suitable" location. And it was simply illegal to take firearms into or out of Dominica.

Alternatively, I suppose you could decide not to declare any firearms to avoid having them confiscated and therefore keep them onboard for use in the unlikely event of an altercation. However, I don't even want to contemplate the hot mess you would be in if you shot, let alone killed, someone—particularly a local—with your now "illegal" firearm.

At any rate, though, it does not make for exciting stories, no guns, and no pirates for us. Boring sounds pretty good!

Hurricanes

We also fielded numerous questions about hurricanes and bad weather in general. Keep in mind that we were cruising for pleasure. We had no hard and fast timelines, on purpose, so if the forecast was bad, we stayed put. If the winds were changing, leaving us in an unprotected anchorage, we moved to a safer spot. Then we stayed put.

Sailors talk about the weather. A *lot*. And with good reason. Picking a good weather window can definitely mean the difference between a comfortable passage and a miserable one. And sometimes, it can mean the difference between life and death. Living and recreating on the water, much of our life revolves around the weather, even at home. Once we moved aboard, this reliance on weather forecasting intensified.

Like any good sailor, we bought and read *Coastal and Offshore Weather: The Essential Handbook* by Chris Parker. Parker, a former cruiser and meteorologist, is the chief forecaster and founder of Marine Weather Center, which provides unparalleled weather forecasting and routing advice to cruisers via daily single-sideband (SSB) voice nets. As technology has improved, he has expanded over the years to provide this information via telephone, email, and text messaging as well. Long before we set sail, we started to listen to Chris's broadcasts to get an idea of the patterns we would see once we left the continental United States and headed for the Bahamas and beyond. While we traveled, we paid for email delivery of his forecasts.

We sailed the "Thorny Path," that is, sailed upwind, from the Bahamas to Turks and Caicos to the north coast of the Dominican Republic and across the Mona Passage to the south coast of Puerto Rico. This route took us against the Trade Winds and against the current, ensuring less-than-ideal sailing conditions. And truly, we were not done "easting" until we reached Antigua.

In addition to weather conditions in the Bahamas, we also paid a lot of attention, prior to heading out, to weather patterns in the Dominican Republic and Puerto Rico. We read and reread Bruce Van Sant's *The Gentleman's Guide to Passages South: The Thornless Path to Windward*. Though I find him an insufferable chauvinist, he does share a wealth of helpful information. All of this ensured we were as safe as we could be, though *comfortable* is not exactly the word I would use to describe these passages.

Learning weather patterns is one thing; hurricanes, however, are an entirely different story. We have the utmost respect for Mother Nature and do not underestimate the deadly power of a hurricane. Hurricane season in the Atlantic and Caribbean officially runs from June 1 through November 30 each year, with most making landfall in September and October. We left in late August 2014 and returned home at the beginning of August two years later, so we were actually out for some or all of three hurricane seasons.

The year we set out, 2014, the National Oceanic and Atmospheric Administration (NOAA) predicted a near-normal or below-normal hurricane season for the Atlantic. Gratefully, that was the case, as there were only eight named storms, the fewest since 1997. Easy peasy. Leaving Massachusetts in late August, we were able to count on good weather forecasting and easy access to it all the way down the East Coast of the United States. We spent September and half of October way up the Potomac River in Washington, DC, which is a great place to hide from a hurricane, if necessary. Then we poked our way down the Intracoastal Waterway from Norfolk, Virginia, to Miami, Florida, which offered plenty of rivers to run up, if need be. Our insurance prohibited us from crossing into Florida until after November 30, the official end of hurricane season, meaning we would not be covered for any damage incurred by a named storm if we did so. Fair enough. We built that timing into our trip south.

In 2015, we again saw a below-average Atlantic hurricane season, with eleven named storms, four of which became hurricanes. We left Florida at the end of December, and by June of 2015, the start of the hurricane season, we were well within running range of Grenada if a hurricane popped up. NOAA keeps a map with over 150 years of historical hurricane tracks. Check it out, and you will see why Grenada was our southernmost destination, as it is outside of the "hurricane box," a roughly 16,000 square mile area that goes from Florida to the middle of Grenada, the southernmost island of the Lesser Antilles.

Again, our insurance dictated that we needed to be below twelve degrees north latitude for the duration of the hurricane season, which is why you will find a rather robust community of cruisers, *Ally Cat* included, in the southern bays of Grenada that time of the year. While we were safely tucked away in Secret Harbor for the bulk of the hurricane season, right where we were supposed to be, tropical storm Erika clobbered Dominica in late August with more than twelve inches of rain, triggering massive mudslides, and hurricane Joaquin, a powerful Category 4 storm, battered the Out Islands of the Bahamas at the end of October. It was startling to return to these beloved places just a few months after our first visit and see firsthand the destruction wrought.

We were only out for a couple of months—the very early months—of the 2016 Atlantic season, which was a very good thing. That year, hurricane activity was well above the previous three years, including fifteen named storms, seven of which became hurricanes, 4 of which were major hurricanes (Category 3 or greater). Though 2016 had an unusually early start, we were back in our home port by August and unaffected by these storms.

We watched in utter disbelief, however, in 2017, as Hurricane Irma, the most powerful Category 5 hurricane on record, made landfall in the Leeward Islands. Irma was followed two weeks later by Maria, a second very powerful Category 5 hurricane. These storms decimated the islands we once called home, albeit for a short period. Dominica, battered once again after just recovering from Erika; Barbuda, with its National Geographic photo-worthy Frigate Bird Sanctuary, was virtually gone; St. Martin had 90 percent of its infrastructure wiped out; the British and US Virgin Islands saw Maria drown what Irma didn't destroy; and Puerto Rico, where their municipal governments were clearly unprepared for a catastrophe of that magnitude.

After these two back-to-back storms, I thought long and hard about what we would have done had we set out in 2017 rather than when we did in 2014. I don't know the answer; however, I do know we were very lucky regarding hurricanes.

CHAPTER 14

MARINA LIFE IN THE CITY

"A ship in harbor is safe, but that is not what ships are built for." — John A. Shedd

Michael took two weeks off from his project in Jacksonville so we could sail *Ally Cat* from Massachusetts to Washington, DC. "Vacation" was kind of an optimistic term for what was essentially a delivery and shakedown cruise. We had over 500 miles to sail, which may not sound like much, but it is *a lot* when you only go about six miles an hour. And *everything* was new to us—the boat, the systems, and our new liveaboard life.

Vacation?

We sailed from Mattapoisett to nearby Cuttyhunk, the Thimble Islands in Connecticut, Port Washington, New York, and down the East River into New York Harbor to Atlantic Highlands, New Jersey. Sailing past the United Nations, with the Chrysler Building looming tall behind and *right* by the Statue of Liberty, etched indelible memories, even though this was our second time.

We sailed overnight from the Highlands to Cape May, New Jersey, ran up the Delaware River and down the Chesapeake and Delaware (C&D) Canal and into the Chesapeake Bay. In the Maryland portion of the Chesapeake Bay, we stopped in the Bohemia River (where we encountered our near-miss lightning strike), Queenstown, and Little Choptank River.

As we headed into Virginia and up the Potomac River, where it flows into the Chesapeake Bay, we stopped in Colonial Beach and Belle Haven Marina in Alexandria—my hometown—before finally arriving at Capital Yacht Club in Washington, DC, where we lived on Dock B for six weeks until Michael finished his project.

Most of the trip to Washington, DC felt very much like any other two-week vacation on the boat, except we were ticking off many more miles than usual, and, on our *very* civilized catamaran, I was not seasick at all. *Ally Cat,* unlike *Wayward,* did not heel over at an uncomfortable angle; we could drink our coffee from regular mugs versus sippy cups, and I was even able to cook dinner while we were underway.

The Atlantic Highlands Municipal Marina, fully reopened a few short months before we arrived, nearly twenty months after Superstorm Sandy. This was a vast improvement over our stop in 2013, as we were bringing *Ally Cat* home from Annapolis, Maryland. Then, the fuel dock had just reopened days before our arrival, and what was left of the marina looked like toothpicks sticking up out of the water.

Trip Planning

As we enjoyed the results of the $20 million reconstruction project in Atlantic Highlands, we planned the next leg of our trip. We mulled it over and eventually decided to sail the New Jersey shore in a single overnight passage again. The weather was good, and our crew was ready.

Before leaving on any passage, in addition to paying copious attention to the weather, we study paper charts for the area and read whatever guidebooks are available. We decide our course and estimate how long the trip *should* take. After that, we head to Zeus, our electronic chart plotter, and set our course and waypoints. Based on the duration of the passage, we determine the departure time and plan our watch schedule.

For short day passages, twelve hours or less, Michael usually maintains the watch while I take care of everything else (meals, Ally, and Michael's needs at the helm). I relieve him for short stints, usually about half an hour at a time. Before we met, Michael almost always single-handed his boats, and he is most comfortable sitting in the captain's chair at the helm and keeping an eye on everything.

Our second overnight passage was one of many fifteen-to thirty-hour passages during our trip, often sailing through the night. To avoid exhaustion, I stood watch for a four-hour stretch at night so my captain could sleep. It's important to note that only one of our passages was longer than thirty hours: our return trip from the Bahamas to the States, when we sailed for fifty-six hours from Double Breasted Cay in the Abacos, Bahamas, to Charleston, South Carolina. We never crossed oceans for days on end; therefore, our watch schedule was generally quite informal compared to that of bluewater cruisers.

I again volunteered for the midnight-to-4 a.m. shift. I went to bed just after dinner, for about four hours, and was ready to take over at midnight. I donned my life jacket and harness, with the attached safety bag containing my PLB, AIS, knife, light, and whistle, and I clipped my tether onto the helm chair. Color me crazy, but I loved standing watch in the middle of the night. With so little ambient light, the stars appeared tantalizingly close, as if I could reach out and touch them. And, with the exception of the noise Ally Cat made pushing us through the water, the world was silent. The peace and solitude were complete and permeated my soul. It was just me and *Ally Cat*. Plus, it was easier for me to see what was around as it was lit up. Generally.

How did I stay awake and attentive during my watch? I started by drinking just enough coffee to be alert for my four-hour watch, yet not so much that I wasn't able to fall asleep after. It was a delicate balance, to be sure. And I read.

Oftentimes, I read cookbooks. Don't laugh; it's one of my favorite pastimes, particularly while watching or listening to baseball. And apparently, while standing watch in the dead of night, enveloped in a sea of darkness. Recipes are generally short enough so I didn't get distracted for too long and could keep a keen watch. Also, given our foray into homeschooling, I read a fair number of textbooks, too. Math, science, and history, in particular. I also read biographies, novels, historical fiction, self-help, devotionals—just about anything. If my eyes were too heavy to read, I listened to music or an audiobook, though with only one earphone, so I could hear the VHF and other sounds. Along the south coast of Puerto Rico, where every passage was an overnight sail, ostensibly when the Trade Winds were at their quietest, I even listened to James Earl Jones read the entire New Testament. On *Ally Cat*, our Kindles were essential equipment.

Michael was usually able to get a solid three to four hours of sleep before relieving me at the helm at four in the morning. He would bring us into port, often as the sun rose.

Disciples of a regular eight-hour sleep every night, the day after an overnight sail was not much fun for either of us. Wasn't it just a few years ago that we could party like rock stars and then get up and actually be productive on a few hours of sleep? Okay, so maybe it was more like thirty-five or forty years ago.

After successfully completing our second overnight sail, we recuperated in Cape May for a day and sailed up the Delaware River, through the C&D Canal into the Chesapeake Bay, and down the entire length of the Chesapeake Bay in four long days. This was when it really started to feel like a "delivery" cruise: the miles covered became our primary goal, not enjoying the journey. We knew there would be more time on another trip to explore the Chesapeake Bay, second only to Buzzards Bay, in my opinion, for the finest sailing in the United States. However, it was tough to simply pass through.

On day eleven, we entered the mouth of the Potomac River, the waterway of my youth, and covered the ninety-five miles up to Washington, DC. I grew up half a mile south of Mount Vernon, George Washington's historic home, on the Potomac River in Alexandria, Virginia, about fifteen miles outside Washington, DC. Sailing wing-on-wing, meaning running downwind with our mainsail on one side of *Ally Cat* and the headsail on the other, up the Potomac River in *my* boat, was intoxicating. Michael said I was grinning from ear to ear.

Anchoring

Other than the week before we left Massachusetts—when *Ally Cat* was tied up to the dock down the street from our house—I had only stayed at marinas three times in my life. The first two were in Nova Scotia on laundry days. The third time was when we launched *Ally Cat* and celebrated our anniversary in Annapolis. We pulled into fuel docks when necessary; however, when we are aboard, we generally spend our nights at anchor. At home, she lives on a mooring in our cove.

We prefer anchoring or picking up a mooring over spending time at marinas. Dropping an anchor is free, which means we can anchor just about anywhere at no cost. Mooring balls are typically less expensive than marinas, which charge per foot based on the boat's length. In our experience, we found that rates at marinas can vary drastically, from reasonably affordable ($1 per foot) to ridiculously expensive ($4.50 per foot, or more).

Our favorite marina was definitely Marina Puerto Bahiá, in the Dominican Republic, at $1 per foot. This $40 per night marina (they have a forty-foot minimum) offered deluxe amenities, including a chic lobby (with fantastic internet) and beautiful grounds to walk, multiple infinity pools, laundry facilities, scrumptious showers, and an *air-conditioned* workout room—a rare find of affordability and opulence.

In January 2015, shortly after our arrival in the Bahamas, we set course for Nassau, the capital and largest city of the Bahamas, located on New Providence Island. Having already visited DC and Miami, we were not particularly keen on exploring more cities. However, we had two compelling reasons for this stopover. First, we needed to purchase the two-stroke engine for our dinghy, and second, for Ally to redeem her Christmas present—a day at Aquaventure.

This colossal water park, part of the Atlantis Bahamas resort, is situated on nearby Paradise Island. At $4.50 per foot, even with the forty-foot minimum, the $180 per day expense was worth it as it included daily access to the resort and Aquaventure, the 141-acre water park with its eleven waterslides, dozens of swimming areas, and mile-long lazy river ride.

In addition to the financial benefits of anchoring, one of the most compelling reasons to be on the hook is to escape the heat. Unless we're anchored in an area with a strong current, *Ally Cat's* bow points into the wind when we're at anchor. This orientation allows the four large overhead hatches to funnel a cooling breeze throughout the vessel. Even during squalls or regular showers in the rainy season, our hatch hoodies keep the rain out while providing decent airflow down below.

Lastly, we appreciate anchoring for its promise of privacy, tranquility, and solitude. While some sailors enjoy the social advantages of docking, we find that our preference for peace aligns harmoniously with our budget.

Marina Shopping

In July, before we set sail, I made a quick trip to DC. The impetus was a mini-college reunion. Though we were flat out at home finishing boat projects, packing up our house, and making final preparations to leave, it provided the perfect opportunity to see friends before we set sail and find a marina we could call home for the six weeks we were in DC. I was making no headway on that task by phone. After our two-week *vacation,* Michael still had two more months of work before beginning his "sabbatical." He was traveling back and forth to Jacksonville, Florida, every other week to wrap up his project. While he was still working and traveling, Ally and I were staying on *Ally Cat,* tied to a dock in a marina.

We immediately ruled out Belle Haven Marina in Virginia. I loved the location, right off the George Washington Memorial Parkway (also known as the GW Parkway, or simply the Parkway) in Alexandria, and we had a friend who kept his boat there; however, there were no facilities for us—specifically showers, laundry, a pump-out station for our holding tank, and internet access. Michael was going to be working from the boat every other week, so internet access was essential. A pump-out for our holding tank, showers, and laundry were pretty important, too.

Our friend from Belle Haven took us across the Potomac River by boat, towing his kids and Ally on an inner tube, to see the swanky National Harbor. Oh my. While it certainly met our needs in terms of showers, laundry, pump-out, and internet, it was a bit excessive. In addition to the marina, which boasts the Capital Wheel—a giant Ferris wheel-type ride with gondolas that soar 180 feet in the air—there are more than thirty restaurants, 150 shops adjacent to the marina, and eight hotels. I even read that a casino would be opening. It was expensive. Not out-of-the-question expensive, but more than we budgeted. It was also in Maryland, on the opposite side of the Potomac River from Virginia, where most of my friends lived, with no public transportation to DC, where we planned to spend a lot of time. We would definitely need a car if we stayed there.

Our next stop was Old Town Alexandria, my old stomping grounds. We checked out the City of Alexandria Marina. The location, at the foot of King Street in the heart of Old Town, was outstanding. Despite an A-plus for location and nice shower facilities, there was no laundry or pump-out, and internet access was questionable. Besides, there were time limitations—maybe a five-day maximum in a single location—that would necessitate us moving around a lot.

Since Old Town was such a great location, we also checked out the Old Dominion Boat Club, the oldest boating club in Virginia. However, they were not at all interested in the likes of us. They only accepted transients who were members of another yacht club. La-de-da.

The next morning, I set off by car to investigate further. I tried really hard to find the Washington Sailing Marina, just north of Old Town and Washington National Airport, passing the Dangerfield Island location on the GW Parkway multiple times. Though the Parkway is one of my favorite roads in the Washington metro area, and I did not mind taking a nostalgic tour down memory lane, after my third pass, I finally stopped in the Theodore Roosevelt Island parking lot to call the marina. Crossing that one off my list and grateful I would *never* have to find it, we couldn't even get into their basin with our forty-six-foot mast. Besides, they explained, they are more of a sailing club than a marina and don't take transients or liveaboards.

As I drove into DC, I struggled with which we were: transients or liveaboards. In addition to the extensive nautical nomenclature, I was learning so many new cruising terms, too. I decided we must be long-term transients, as we were definitely not *moving* to DC to *live* on our boat. Or maybe we were short-term liveaboards?

There had been talk pretty much my entire life about renovating the DC waterfront area. Amazingly, in the summer of 2014, work *finally* started on what is now known as The Wharf. I was thrilled that Washington was going to capitalize on the magnificent stretch of waterfront that perpetually failed to realize its full potential; however, the timing could not have been worse for us.

My first stop in DC was at Gangplank Marina. From the moment we started talking about spending a couple of months in the DC area, Gangplank Marina was where I envisioned we'd stay. The location was perfect: right across the street from Arena Stage in southwest DC, an easy walk to the National Mall via L'Enfant Plaza, where we could hop on the Metro, too. With a definitive bounce in my step, I located the harbormaster's office, confident I would be able to make reservations for September and October.

No dice.

Damn, the construction! The harbormaster explained they lost a dock in the consolidation required to complete Phase I, so they were not accepting any transients.

"Hum, how about if we came in as liveaboards?" I mused.

We ran through several scenarios to see what might work. In the end, as helpful and friendly as the harbormaster was, unfortunately, Gangplank was not a viable option.

Following the harbormaster's suggestions and directions, I visited James Creek Marina, not far away in southeast DC. Though they would accept transients, they did not have a pump-out, so we would have to move the boat every time our holding tanks were full. And it was not in the best neighborhood.

Gangplank's harbormaster also mentioned Capital Yacht Club. Given my experience with Old Dominion Boat Club, I was not terribly optimistic. However, as my last stop, it was also my last hope. Sitting in a long line of traffic in the middle of a construction zone, where my handy dandy GPS led me, with less than a quarter mile until I reached my destination, I pulled into a shabby two-story parking deck. I figured, correctly, I could get there more quickly on foot.

Capital Yacht Club is located in southwest DC, adjacent to the historic Maine Avenue Fish Market, the oldest continuously operating fish market in the country. And it was ground zero for Phase 1 of The Wharf.

I walked past construction fences to check out the facility. As it was Sunday, the office was closed, and I wasn't able to find anyone around. I noted the big clubhouse, the nice outside deck with grills and picnic tables, and the four long docks, and dinghy dock, all behind locked gates. It looked promising. If they would take us.

As I was leaving, contemplating living there for a couple of months, warming to the idea despite the construction, a man with two kids a little younger than Ally pulled in and started unloading the car. I mustered my courage and approached them.

"Do you keep your boat here?" I asked.

"Yes, we just moved it to Dock A last week," he replied.

Although they were still new to Capital Yacht Club, I bombarded him with questions. He was able to tell me about the clubhouse—nice laundry and shower facilities, a bar, and a function room. And he was able to pump out their holding tank without leaving moving the boat.

"I'm not sure about internet access on the docks," he admitted somewhat sheepishly. "I come to the boat to escape work."

It looked more and more promising. Armed with the office manager's name, thanks to my new friend, and a plan to call first thing Monday morning, I rejoined the reunion festivities. The next morning, though she hemmed and hawed a bit, given the upheaval caused by the construction, the office manager agreed to take our reservation at Capital Yacht Club. For two weeks. After that, she could make no promises. She agreed to reevaluate the construction progress to decide if we would be able to stay through mid-October. Plus, she confirmed there was reliable internet all the way down each of the four docks.

Satisfied we had a home when we arrived in DC, and moderately confident we could convince them to let us stay through October—I was not above bribery—I checked that item off my list.

Our Marina Home

As we sailed toward Capital Yacht Club, we anchored off Bell Haven Marina in Alexandria, Virginia, before proceeding into DC. Michael and Ally indulged me in a couple of nostalgic days exploring my old stomping grounds. As we headed ashore for a walk on the bike trail along the Parkway, learner's permit in hand, I drove the dinghy ashore.

Driving boats is just not intuitive for me, and in those early days, I found myself concentrating so hard to make sure my speed was consistent and that I turned the tiller the correct way that I had to remind myself to breathe. In and out. I managed to maneuver around the boat house with ease.

"No problem, you're doing great," I cheered myself on. And I pulled up to the dock like a pro, as if I had been doing it my whole life.

Radiating confidence, I grabbed my bag and hopped out of the dinghy onto a very wobbly finger pier. Or *almost* onto the pier. Both my bag and I took an unplanned plunge into the Potomac River. Apparently, I overestimated my abilities. Thankfully, I was not hurt. Humiliated but not hurt. As I emerged from the water, picking seaweed out of my hair and teeth, Michael and Ally stood by silently, waiting to see if I was going to laugh or cry. Happily for all, I chose to laugh. We set out for our walk. It was beastly hot, and guess who was cool as a cucumber? Yep, me, freshly out of the river after my swim. It was nearly twenty minutes before water stopped squishing out of my sneakers.

I was reminded that going with the flow is always a better choice than freaking out, regardless of the situation. Having a sense of humor is so important, too, and I especially value my ability to laugh at myself. Another lesson that was hammered home that day was this: since I lived on a boat, if I wanted to keep something dry, I had to put it in a dry bag, even if I didn't plan on swimming. We bought high-quality dry bags in a variety of sizes. There were small ones for the contents of my purse (though, honestly, I quickly transitioned to a "cruiser's wallet," also known as a Ziplock baggie), midsize ones to hold our laptop, Kindles or other electronics, and large and extra-large ones for laundry. Transfers seemed to be when I was most vulnerable—going from the boat to the dinghy or from the dinghy to the boat and from the dinghy to the dock or shore and back into the dinghy. Though I was pretty sure I'd take a few other unplanned swims, I only had one more in the entire two years! I gave Ally and Michael a good laugh, had a good laugh myself, and then added those clothes to the laundry I was on my way to wash.

Sailing under the Woodrow Wilson Memorial Bridge, which spans the Potomac River between Virginia and Maryland, another unforgettable moment for me, we arrived in DC and got *Ally Cat* settled into her slip on Dock B at Capital Yacht Club—*home* for the next six weeks.

We stopped into the office to say "hello" and checked out the facilities, which were every bit as nice as we hoped. After spending two weeks on the boat, the next order of business was to stretch our legs and explore our new neighborhood. We walked out of the marina onto Maine Avenue, passing the Fish Market, East Potomac Park, and Hains Point. Within fifteen minutes, we were climbing the steps of the Thomas Jefferson Memorial.

New Neighbors in a New Neighborhood

Before leaving Massachusetts, one of the final items to check off my list was what to do with my cars. We had already decided to keep Michael's reliable Ford Taurus, taking it off the road, and canceling insurance and registration in the hope it would still run two years later—a gamble that paid off. I was driving a ten-year-old 2004 Honda Accord. Though my car ran fine, we weren't wholly confident about its long-term reliability. Should we keep it? Should we sell it? We tossed around the idea of driving the Honda to DC and selling it before we headed south, debating the pros and cons. In the end, within days of our departure, my car developed an alarming engine clunk. I made the executive decision and sold it.

I eagerly embraced our new life in the city. Without a vehicle, we relied on public transportation, like so many other Washingtonians. We would have had a very different experience in DC had we kept the car. Though having a car would have been quite handy on many occasions, I am grateful for our decision. Instead of popping out to the suburbs I knew, we were forced to be much more creative to find what we needed right in DC, preferably within walking distance. This resourcefulness proved to be a skill we relied on throughout our trip.

We continued our walk around the Tidal Basin to the Washington Monument. Just beyond the Jefferson Memorial, within twenty minutes of *Ally Cat's* new home, was the National Mall, which includes more than one hundred monuments and memorials. The Mall is flanked by the museums of the Smithsonian Institute, the world's largest museum and research complex. At the eastern end of the Mall is the United States Capitol, and to the north is the White House. Nearby were the Supreme Court, the National Archives, and the Bureau of Engraving and Printing, among many other landmarks. We had arrived in boatschooling paradise.

The day after we tied up at Capital Yacht Club, Michael hopped in an Uber to Washington National Airport just across the river and flew back to Jacksonville for work, where they still had *no* idea what we were up to. The following day, my forty-sixth birthday, Ally started fifth grade. In addition to the Mall and the Smithsonian, we explored our new neighborhood, as well. Just down Maine Avenue, past Arena Stage, where it becomes M Street, we found our local grocery and drug stores and our closest Metro station.

Nearby, we found a library. Honestly, Ally and I have a sixth sense and can find a library anywhere. We checked it out, hoping it would give us a place, other than the boat, for school some days and be a source of honest-to-goodness books. I loved my Kindle, but there is nothing like the feel—and smell—of a *real* book in my hands. We discovered all we needed to do was bring our marina paperwork, basically a lease of sorts, and they would issue us library cards. The next day we became card-carrying DC Public Library members.

Once we arrived in DC, and throughout the trip, both grocery shopping and laundry consisted of long treks with heavy loads. I brought my Nantucket Beach Buggy since we already owned it. Think of a folding utility cart, you know, a granny cart, on steroids. Intended to schlep coolers, chairs, umbrellas, toys, and towels to the beach, it was durable, carried *a lot,* and had all-terrain wheels. It may have been a bit extreme for the city; however, it was fantastic for schlepping groceries and laundry. I had quite a few gals on my way to and from the grocery store comment on my nifty setup. My buggy made it all the way to Grenada before rust caught up with us, and it lost a wheel. Sadly, I haven't been able to find the same Nantucket Beach Buggy in stores or online since, though I think I will try one of those heavy-duty collapsible wagons when we venture out next. I saw quite a few cruisers using them.

One of the most rewarding aspects of our time in DC was becoming part of a cruising community, a concept previously unknown to me. We were no longer figuring everything out on our own. On Ally's first day of boatschool, which happened to also be my birthday, we met our dock neighbors. When we met the Hackneys in 2014, Tanya, Jay, and their *five* kids had lived aboard *Take Two,* a forty-eight-foot wooden catamaran, full-time for more than six years. Tanya and Jay tossed off their dock lines about the time we took our first RV trip when they were still a family of six. Their youngest had *never* lived on land! They sold their land-based house and took the plunge into the cruising life, barely looking back. Jay's technical career allowed him to work remotely long before it became fashionable during COVID. Tanya had homeschooled all of her kids all of their lives in anticipation of their eventual move aboard.

Not only did we immediately become friends, Tanya also taught me *so much* about living and cooking aboard and boatschooling. I will forever consider her my birthday present, sent straight from God. Plus, their crew included ten–year–old Sarah, who became fast friends with ten-year-old Ally.

For Ally and me, one of the most challenging aspects of setting sail was leaving our friends. However, the crew of *Take Two* taught us that we would find exactly what we needed when we needed it. In our marina, there were *four* other boats with girls about Ally's age living on boats with their families. With our new neighbors, we found camaraderie and community, filling our days with field trips and play dates, cocktails and potlucks, and even one memorable moms' night in. These more experienced fellow cruisers fueled our imagination about what was to come and provided guidance in the necessary skills to get us there.

CHAPTER 15

A GARDENER WITHOUT
A GARDEN

"For those who have come to grow, the whole world is a garden. For those who have come to learn, the whole world is a university." —M.R. Bawa Muhaiyaddeen

My favorite smell is dirt—although the proper term is actually soil, given its living nature. I love the way it smells; I love the way it feels. I particularly love that each and every spring, it brings forth shoots from buried bulbs, tubers, and rhizomes producing brave snowdrops and crocus, eternally optimistic daffodils, and tulips and lilies in a rainbow of colors. I love the promise the most impossibly tiny seed buried in the soil holds to become nourishment served with love on my dinner table. Sugar snap peas, green beans, cucumber, tomatoes, squash, carrots—I love them all.

I prefer to live my life outside rather than in. Given the choice, I will always opt for yard work over housework. Mopping floors or mowing the lawn? Mowing, hands down. And there is no contest between dishes and weeding. Not only do I love the glory tasks of gardening—harvesting baskets full of fresh produce all summer, picking and eating berries until my belly aches, cutting blooms for a summer centerpiece—I take great pleasure in the mundane, as well. Weeding, mulching, mowing, and pruning are forms of meditation for me. I find working in my gardens to be the best therapy for my body, mind, and soul. I am simply more *me* in the garden than virtually anywhere else on earth.

As Ally approached her first birthday, she ventured into food. Not baby food, but *real* food. My job, as I saw it, was to put healthy food in front of her and let her choose what and how much to eat. And I took that job quite seriously. As Ally expanded her palate, food became an important topic to me, too. I wanted to know exactly where our food came from and how it had been grown or raised. Increasingly, we were reducing processed foods and opting for whole foods and organics to avoid unnecessary hormones, antibiotics, and other chemicals.

When possible, we began buying our food from local organic farms. Ever the trendsetters, we experimented with a meat CSA (Community Supported Agriculture) early in their heyday, supporting local farmers financially and enjoying a variety of grass-fed and pasture-raised meats. We even bought our own piglet and calf one year that were raised by neighbors. As we watched these animals grow, we became quasi-experts in the processing and use of all parts of the animals. That was a pretty radical concept considering I was a vegetarian all through my twenties!

I experimented with an organic vegetable CSA, as well. My goal was to use every single thing I brought home from the farm each week. Who knew we loved pea greens so much? And while celeriac, the hairy root cousin of celery, may never be a fan favorite in our house, kohlrabi, Swiss chard, and kale are now regulars on our table, thanks to that experiment!

About this time, my book club read Barbara Kingsolver's *Animal, Vegetable, Miracle: A Year of Food Life*. To say it changed my life is an understatement. As I read the story of the author's family's attempt to eat only locally grown food for an entire year, I realized I could add "local" to our organic whole food.

While I was searching the internet to figure out how to use pea greens and celeriac from our share, I started my own garden. The following year, when I again signed up for the CSA, I took the idea one step further: instead of paying upfront, I opted for a "work share." In exchange for our share of the harvest, I committed to work on the farm each week during the growing season.

Armed with a treasure trove of knowledge from my season on the farm, I was eager to expand my gardens. Michael helped me realize my dream: fourteen four-foot-by-fourteen-foot raised beds, with two-foot-wide walkways between each and around the borders. Aesthetics are important to me; my gardens are a canvas for my art.

With close to a decade of dirt therapy in my gardens, as we began planning our trip, it was only natural that a common question for me was, "What about your gardens?" I can't count the number of times I was asked if I would grow herbs and vegetables on board. I did not. However, it didn't take long to discover what would fill the gardening void: cooking for my crew.

We are often asked what we eat on the boat—and often in a tone that leads me to believe they expect the answer may be "peanut butter and jelly." Three meals a day. The reality is that we eat very well on board. While sailing, there is *a lot* of time to think about food, and at anchor, there is ample time, as well, to prepare tasty meals. Prior to our two-year trip, we sailed during the summer months, when fresh produce was always abundant. And because our vacations were generally just a week or two, we easily stocked up on good healthy food before we left, supplementing at local grocery stores along the way, if necessary. We always ate very similarly to how we ate at home: bagels or yogurt and granola with fruit for breakfast; some sort of a salad or sandwich for lunch; and generally a simple meal of a meat or fish, a vegetable, and a starch for dinner.

I read *The Boat Galley Cookbook,* cover-to-cover, between Massachusetts and Washington, DC. Laugh if you must, but I am willing to bet you have missed a considerable amount of useful information located in the first few chapters of cookbooks as you flipped ahead to the much more seductive recipe sections. And you have *definitely* missed information that is worth its weight in gold from Carolyn Shearlock and Jan Irons in *The Boat Galley Cookbook* if you skipped the first six chapters: Boat Cooking *is* Different, Equipping a Galley, Provisioning, Food Storage, Food Substitutions, and Measurements and Conversions (including metric conversations).

Though I knew of some from Michael, I learned about so many more foods that conventional (that is, land-based) wisdom insists need to be refrigerated but really don't. Considering fridge space is quite limited, I no longer squandered precious real estate on condiments: soy sauce, Worcestershire sauce, jams, salad dressings, ketchup, mustard, or even mayonnaise! Eggs didn't command shelf space in my fridge either, regardless of whether they had been washed or not or previously refrigerated or not.

How about thermos cooking? Have you heard of that? Yep, I learned about it by reading my cookbook, too. Thanks to Carolyn Shearlock, who calls a thermos the "cruiser's Crock-Pot," I learned how to make my own yogurt! We enjoyed fresh yogurt for the entire two years, with the exception of when we were in the French islands, as their yogurt was too delicious not to buy.

Plus, a thermos is "good for foods that require long simmering, as it saves propane, keeps heat out of the boat, and frees you to do something else while the food cooks," as Shearlock points out in chapter 2, Equipping a Galley. It's a brilliant idea for pasta, rice, couscous, and even dried beans. I ordered my thermos the first day we were at Capital Yacht Club and began experimenting with new recipes right away. Ally made her way through two of the last three chapters, Quick Breads, Muffins, and Biscuits and Sweet Tooth, honing her baking skills. She even made a pineapple upside-down cake for her own birthday dessert potluck when she turned twelve!

I also learned, from my trusty *Boat Galley Cookbook,* about using a pizza stone in our tiny boat oven to disperse the heat a bit more evenly. And to turn pans a hundred and eighty degrees halfway through the baking time so as not to burn foods. I wish I'd read that part *before* I experimented with granola, as there is not much in the way of temperature control either. Our oven is either on or off and generally cooks at about 350 degrees. My granola, wanting a long slow cook at a low temp, sadly had to be chiseled off the pan. I did figure out baking granola in the oven, but it tasted *so* good there was no thought of saving it for breakfast, and it was gone the next day. Luckily, I was saved by Tanya's recipe for muesli, basically dry granola, which we enjoyed with our fresh yogurt. It consisted of oats, shredded coconut, cinnamon, salt, dried fruit, and a variety of nuts and seeds—sliced almonds, pecans, walnuts, pumpkin, and/or sunflower seeds, depending on what was available. Other than the Dutch side of St. Martin, also known as Sint Maarten, nuts and seeds were nearly impossible to buy—or they were so cost prohibitive in such small quantities that it just did not make sense to buy them. Any time we had visitors, if they asked what they could bring for us, we generally arranged for them to bring boat parts, some sort of homeschool supplies, and about ten pounds of nuts!

I have a confession: Michael actually had *multiple* online boyfriends! In addition to Walt, he also corresponded with Danny for months before we set sail. Danny and his wife, Dominique, were headed to the Bahamas from Canada aboard their Gemini, *JessyMo,* with their kids, on a similar schedule to ours. Danny noted that our kids were roughly the same age and asked if we could meet along the way. We were finally in the same place at the same time in the Tidewater area of Virginia. For the last three weeks of Michael's project, we stayed in a marina right next to Hampton University, having moved *Ally Cat* from DC so we were poised to jump into the Atlantic Intracoastal Waterway (ICW) in Norfolk as soon as he was finished. *JessyMo* was anchored not far away, in the Elizabeth River in Norfolk, getting ready to do the same thing. One memorable evening, we took an Uber from Hampton to Norfolk, where Danny picked us up at the waterfront for an entertaining evening aboard *JessyMo.*

The kids, all crammed into one of the quarter berths playing games (never mind their kids spoke no English and Ally spoke no French) had one giant giggle fest all night long. Michael and Danny, naturally, talked boats all evening. Meanwhile, Dominique taught me how to bake the most heavenly bread! Two days later, as we entered our very first lock in the ICW, Deep Creek Lock, at mile marker 10.5, my very first loaf of bread came out of the oven! Yum. I have shared that recipe, a four-ingredient no-knead wonder that even suggests a nap while rising, with countless cruisers, not to mention landlubbers, as well! Think you may need it, too?

Classic White Bread

(from Dominique on *JessyMo*, October 2014)

3 ¼ cup unbleached flour

2 ¼ tsp rapid-rise yeast

½ - 1 tsp salt (sea or kosher)

1 ½ cups warm water (about 100 degrees)

Mix dry ingredients together. Add water. Mix with a wooden spoon 40 times. Dough will be sticky. Cover with saran wrap. Wait ... wait ... wait. About two hours. Nap! Using a spatula, slide dough into a greased bread pan to make a formed loaf. Otherwise, flour hands and form dough into desired shape to make dinner, hamburger or sandwich rolls, a baguette, a pizza crust, or focaccia, which is quite tasty brushed with olive oil and topped with fresh or dried herbs. Bake at 350 for 45-60 minutes, turning once halfway through baking time.

While we were in DC, Tanya introduced me to Thrive Foods, a full line of freeze-dried foods. She'd used them for years when *Take Two* was in the Bahamas, particularly in the Out Islands, where the availability of fresh fruit, veggies, meat, and dairy was completely dependent on Mail Boat schedules. I placed a big order, which arrived in Florida before we left for the Bahamas, consisting of the following items: eggs, butter, sour cream, shredded mozzarella cheese, shredded cheddar cheese, black beans, pinto beans, crumbled sausage, ground beef, beef cubes, blueberries, strawberries, pineapple, tomato paste, celery, mixed peppers, mushrooms, peas, and corn. I also ordered diced tomatoes and cilantro; however, both of those items were back ordered and wouldn't be shipped in time.

I wish I had learned about Thrive Foods earlier in my planning, as it would have been helpful to have headed for the Bahamas knowing then what I learned in the Bahamas. What did I learn? I would not buy eggs or butter again, as both were readily available everywhere we sailed, from the Bahamas to the Turks & Caicos, Dominican Republic, Puerto Rico, and the Virgins, and from St. Martin down to Grenada. Cheddar cheese, too. Both the sour cream and shredded mozzarella cheese were *big* hits! The mozzarella cheese absolutely made the meal when I made Dominique's classic white bread for pizza crust. And sour cream, along with the corn, was always a welcome addition to staples such as chili, chicken tortilla soup, fish tacos, and burritos. Once our Thrive sour cream ran out, I experimented with an alternate method suggested in *The Boat Galley Cookbook*, my cooking bible, using canned cream, vinegar, and water—all ingredients readily available.

That experiment was a resounding success, though I would have been happy to have more Thrive sour cream powder on hand, too!

I was disappointed the cilantro was not available as it would have been a *wonderful* addition, with the sour cream, to all of our Mexican favorites. On the rare occasions when I found culantro, the more robustly flavored cousin of cilantro found in the Caribbean, we devoured it, adding it to all of our Mexican favorites, as well as guacamole and salsa. Yum. I miss the ginormous avocados and guacamole just thinking about them!

Though I was disappointed I wasn't able to get Thrive diced tomatoes, canned tomatoes were readily available where we sailed, also, though freeze-dried tomatoes weigh much less than their canned counterparts. However, we loaded our girl with so much stuff—spare parts, tools, toiletries, etc.—that the water line went up a good two inches. Clearly, while we gave lip service to weight, we had not paid much attention to it. We may not have sailed very fast, but we ate well!

I found that I did not use the mushrooms and peas much, though I found the celery and mixed peppers were phenomenal when I whipped up conch cakes in the Bahamas, where conch is plentiful, and fresh veggies are scarce. If you sail in colder climes, the peas and mushrooms would probably come in handy in soups and stews. I never did try to reconstitute the tomato paste powder, as canned paste and sauce were also readily available.

All of the fruit was terrific, particularly in the Bahamas, where fruit was scarce. In fact, our stash didn't make it past the Bahamas. Though it was not a problem finding fruit from the Dominican Republic down to Grenada, we really wished we had more Thrive fruit when we were back in the Bahamas on our way north, particularly blueberries. Michael and I both *loved* the dried blueberries mixed into our homemade yogurt and dry granola. After the freeze-dried fruit was gone, when fresh fruit wasn't available, raisins or craisins were a decent substitute. I guess. Surprisingly, we were able to get bananas and apples (which, although they were pricey, stored well, and we all loved them) all the way from the States to Grenada. And mangos. Don't even get me started on mangos. Ann Vanderhoof wrote a book called *An Embarrassment of Mangoes: A Caribbean Interlude.* She's written a chronicle of their journey, which was not dissimilar to ours, with the perfect title. When mangoes are in season, they are beyond plentiful–an embarrassment, if you will!

Of the meats, we wished we had brought more cans of the crumbled sausage, as that is what we used and liked the most. I would add a fairly small amount (about half a cup) to chili or red sauce or on a pizza for a great pop of flavor. Once we ran out of freeze-dried sausage, I was often able to find bulk sausage. I would cook it in large batches and freeze it in half-cup portions. Of course, not only did this method use precious freezer space and propane, it was also more time-consuming and heated up the boat.

I would skip the freeze-dried beans, both black and kidney, as dried beans of all types were readily available. Most of the time, I soaked the dried beans overnight, and the pressure cooker shortened the cooking time considerably, or I used my handy dandy thermos to avoid heating up the boat. I cheated and kept some canned beans on board when they were available, and we had room, particularly refried beans for burritos, as making them from scratch was fairly labor intensive, even if they were sublime.

As an aside, Thrive Foods was the only producer of freeze-dried products that I knew about in 2014 as we prepared to leave the United States. At the time, their products were only sold by independent distributors and were not inexpensive. The last time I did a bit of research on Amazon, it appeared Thrive had plenty of competitors, many of whom likely make very similar products, making them easily available. And *much* less expensive.

I quizzed Tanya with question after question about cooking with Thrive Foods, and she shared her secrets with me time and time again. For Christmas, she surprised me with my very own copy of her cookbook, *The Galley Goddess*, which she had written featuring Thrive Foods. Galley Goddess is truly the perfect description for Tanya.

CHAPTER 16

WE'RE CRUISING

"In the end, we only regret the chances we didn't take."
—*Lewis Carroll*

Michael finished his project on November 14, after a one-week delay, just in time for the temperature in Hampton, Virginia, to drop twenty degrees overnight. Once he was no longer straddling both the work and cruising worlds, cold notwithstanding, it was time to get moving. The only way to get to warmer weather was to head south.

When we were growing up, both our families hosted Thanksgiving dinner every year. We each knew that we wanted to continue the tradition. When Michael and I met in 2001, my family was still figuring out Thanksgiving, as neither my sisters nor I had married, and we were spread out across the country, living in Tennessee, California, and Alaska. I hosted Thanksgiving a couple of times while I still lived in Virginia, but nothing seemed to happen consistently from year to year with my family.

Michael's mom was ready to pass the baton, and Michael was a willing successor, having just moved into his newly built house, his first home. Michael and I started dating in late September, and in early November, he asked if I wanted to come to Massachusetts for Thanksgiving.

"I'd like you to meet my family," he cooed. "And help me host for the first time in my new house."

Ah. "Um, sure." Little did I know this meant meeting close to twenty of his relatives all at once—or that this man did not own so much as a serving platter.

We took Thanksgiving week off work to prepare. On your mark, get set, shop! Not exactly a sport either of us enjoys. We bought roasting pans and serving dishes, hot pads and dish towels, wine glasses, and knives, tablecloths and silverware, measuring cups and mixing bowls, colanders and coffee mugs, and Tupperware and baking dishes. I am definitely a list gal, and this mission, all to be completed in less than a week, took all of my list-making skills.

Not only did the kitchen need to be stocked from A to Z, the rest of the house did as well. At forty-three, Michael had never been married nor owned a house. In fact, he owned so little that the two times he quit the "real" world and took off sailing, he stored his half dozen or so boxes in his Mom's basement. He was pretty much a confirmed bachelor if ever there was one.

Add to our lists a king-size bed for the master bedroom, and sheets, pillows, a comforter, and some decorative throw pillows. (Michael will never understand the need for throw pillows.) To his credit, he did have a bed, a queen-size futon that was destined to become the guest bed. Bath towels and shower curtains, hand towels and soap dispensers, bath mats, and door mats. I even made, as in *sewed*, curtains for the kitchen and bathroom windows.

It may have been *his* house, but it was *my* stuffing. Actually, it was my Grandma Fain's stuffing, complete with all of her old-fashioned steps. Consequently, we added a hand-cranked meat grinder for making bread crumbs to the list. The night before our feast, I turned on the broiler to toast up two loaves of bread—there would be no store-bought bread crumbs for Gram!

Suddenly, I noticed a peculiar smell. Oh, no! The knobs on the stove were melting off. I acted quickly and turned off the oven. It seemed that 'Broil' was not an option.

"Must be a problem with the gas-to-propane conversion," Michael said. All righty, then. So, I toasted two loaves of bread in the toaster oven, which took considerably more time.

The next morning, my sweet nieces-to-be, Betsy and Becca, ages twelve and ten, came over to watch Macy's Thanksgiving Day Parade while grinding the toast, celery, and onions for the stuffing. I loved sharing this annual tradition with them more than twenty years ago. And God bless my sister-in-law Beth, who came over late in the morning, once the turkey and stuffing were safely in the oven, to take me for a walk before meeting sixteen more family members.

In hindsight, planning and executing that first Thanksgiving was the perfect way to learn that we work really well together. Both of us are good planners; we knew how to divide and conquer when necessary and team up when it made more sense. We also discovered that we have very similar decision-making styles: quick and sure, with virtually no second-guessing or revisiting a decision once it's been made. We make the best decisions we can with the information available at the time and then proceed.

Little did we know that those very skills were exactly what we needed to plan and execute this trip. Actually, they serve us quite well in life in general.

That first Thanksgiving in Michael's new house was a resounding success, melted knobs notwithstanding. By the next Thanksgiving, Michael and I were engaged, and I had moved to Massachusetts from Nashville, Tennessee. We continued to host our favorite holiday for the next twelve years until we set off in *Ally Cat*. Some years we had as few as fifteen; one year, we had twenty-five, which we deemed our maximum capacity. And if you look closely, the knobs on the stove still bear melted scars from my first—and only— attempt to broil bread for my stuffing.

As we started to think about Thanksgiving 2014, our first major holiday aboard *Ally Cat*, and I thought about the menu, I asked Ally and Michael what foods were important to them, what made Thanksgiving *Thanksgiving* to them. For Ally, it was onion dip and Ruffles potato chips. She also needed a pumpkin pie for it to truly feel like Thanksgiving. Predictably, Michael needed turkey and apple pie. For me, Grandma Fain's stuffing was the key; however, the old-fashioned way I still liked to prepare it wasn't at all practical on a boat. Alas, we wouldn't be able to watch the Macy's Thanksgiving Day Parade while hand-grinding our bread crumbs.

My happy memories of stuffing aside, I realized that I wholly enjoy the preparations and love that go into serving my family on Thanksgiving Day. Though it would be strange to cook for only three, I came up with our menu:

- Salami, Cheese, and Cracker Platter
- Onion Dip and Ruffles Potato Chips
- Smoked Turkey Breast
- Garlic Mashed Potatoes
- Gravy
- Sautéed Tarragon Carrots
- Homemade Rolls
- Mini Pumpkin Pies
- Apple Pie
- Homemade Cranberry Relish

The menu planned, I created a shopping list. Since we were still in the States, it was not a problem to find everything on our list, including walnuts and cranberries, canned pumpkin and sour cream, pie crusts, and Ruffles potato chips. I shopped the Sunday before Thanksgiving in Wilmington, North Carolina. A childhood friend of Michael's and his wife live there, so I did not even have to figure out where the grocery store was, how to get there, or how I would carry everything back to *Ally Cat*. While the boys watched football, running multiple loads of laundry through their washer and dryer, Beth and I simply drove to the grocery store.

Finding a turkey that would fit in the refrigerator for the next four days and our toaster-oven-sized oven was not an easy task, but I was successful. And I did manage to crack myself up in the poultry section as I read aloud what was in each case, "Duck ... duck ... goose!" I stood giggling uncontrollably as other shoppers gave me a wide berth. I know, I am easily amused. After checking everything off my list, we were ready for our first Thanksgiving aboard *Ally Cat*.

We started to calculate where we might physically be to celebrate Thanksgiving. It looked as if Charleston, South Carolina, would be the place. Located at mile marker 469.3 on the ICW, Charleston is about halfway from Norfolk, Virginia (mile marker 0.0) to Miami, Florida (mile marker 1089.0). The port city's rich history made it an attractive to take a few days off and explore, too.

Though it was still chilly, the temperatures were finally warm enough to anchor in both the Calabash River and the Minim River between Wilmington and Charleston. Just barely warm enough. After four ridiculously soggy days and more than 180 cloudy miles on the ICW, the sun finally shone as we sailed into Charleston Harbor. Let the drying out and cooking begin!

Charleston City Marina was full, so we opted to stay at nearby Ashley Marina, as we were able to get into downtown Charleston on foot. We enjoyed a much-needed walk from the marina, along the waterfront, through the Battery, and into the historic French Quarter. After a enchanting dinner at Poogan's Porch, one of Charleston's oldest restaurants, we caved into temptation and enjoyed decadent treats at Kaminsky's Dessert Cafe, a dessert institution.

Before we left home, I packed a holiday bin to take with us. In it, I included a few meaningful items to use for each holiday. For Thanksgiving, this included the turkey place mat from Ally's toddler days and Mr. and Mrs. Pilgrim, small figurines that my sister-in-law gave me on that very first Thanksgiving I shared with Michael. Once these items dressed up our salon table, it started to feel more like Thanksgiving. I was ready to cook. It was still chilly, and I welcomed having the oven on all day heating up *Ally Cat*.

We did not have any pie pans aboard; they just did not make the cut for our limited galley gear. Given the size of our oven and limited counter space, I had to be creative with my pies. I planned to make both the apple and pumpkin pies into mini-pies, baking them in my six-cup jumbo muffin pan. I started with the pumpkin pies. Fresh out of the oven, they looked great; however, when I tried to get them out of the pan, they did not come out easily. I decided to leave them where they were—in the pan—so they would look decent, at least until I served them. I went to Plan B for the apple pie. Have you ever heard of an apple pie loaf? Me neither! I made the apple pie in my bread pan, and though it looked a little funny, it was delicious. It was quite the deep-dish apple pie, actually.

After the pies were done and the smoked turkey breast was in the oven, I had way too much fun creating my Tom Turkey appetizer out of salami and cheddar cheese slices and crackers. It was almost too cute to eat. Cranberry relish, garlic mashed potatoes, sautéed tarragon carrots—it was *much* harder to get everything ready at the same time with our miniature oven and only two burners. For our dinner rolls, I made Dominique's classic white bread and simply shaped the dough into small individual-sized rolls rather than into a traditional loaf.

We learned an unfortunate lesson about gravy: though smoked turkey breast tastes delicious, without the tasty drippings from a whole bird, it is impossible to make good gravy. Whatever you do, trust me on this, *do not* attempt to make gravy with flour and chicken broth. It is not a viable substitute for the good stuff. If we're ever in that situation again, rest assured I will either buy canned gravy or use one of those handy packets. We also discovered that leftovers, without the luxury of a microwave, are a bit more of a challenge to reheat, though not impossible.

The biggest lesson we learned, though, was that it does not matter what we eat or where we are, what really makes Thanksgiving *Thanksgiving* is spending the day with the ones we love. We missed our extended family back in

Massachusetts, but our Crew of Three had a very memorable Thanksgiving that first year out cruising.

What happened to the whole gang we usually hosted for Thanksgiving? Thankfully, Michael's cousin hosted the two years we were gone. We were a little concerned we might have lost hosting privileges or have to agree to an every-other-year schedule of hosting; however, it turns out he was happy to pinch hit and was equally happy we wanted to host again.

We finally thawed out as we moved further south in Florida. After St. Augustine and Titusville, we headed for Harbortown Marina in Ft. Pierce, where *Take Two* was docked after returning to Florida from Washington, DC. We anchored for the night about thirty-five miles north of Ft. Pierce, anxious to see our friends the next afternoon.

***

BEEP! BEEP! BEEP! Our engine started overheating right after we got underway. We stopped and dropped the anchor. Michael went to work troubleshooting. He reached into the raw water strainer and pulled out a wad of seaweed. It must have been clogged, not allowing seawater to flow through to cool the engine. We weighed the anchor, and we were off again.

BEEP! BEEP! BEEP! What? Guess it wasn't the raw water strainer. We anchored again just outside of the channel. Michael checked the raw water impeller and found it was missing a fin. He found the spare part and replaced it. We weighed the anchor, and we were off *again*.

BEEP! BEEP! BEEP! We anchored *again.* Michael went looking for the missing fin. Finding it quickly, just outside the heat exchanger, he thought *that* must be the problem. We weighed the anchor yet again, and we were off yet again.

BEEP! BEEP! BEEP! Down with the anchor, *yet again,* Michael saw coolant in the bilge, indicating we had a leak on the freshwater side. Frustrated, though he has mad mechanical skills, he knew whatever was wrong with the engine was not in his wheelhouse to fix.

Debating whether we should call TowBoatUS, we realized there was a great north breeze, twenty to twenty-five knots, so we decided to sail the twenty-five to thirty miles to Ft. Pierce. *Ally Cat* was a sailboat after all.

We had a pleasingly uneventful sail. There was only one bridge to deal with: the North Ft. Pierce Bascule Bridge, right before our turn-off to go into the marina. We called way ahead via the VHF to let the bridge controller know that we were disabled and under sail only. We could see that it was open when we called, even though we were far enough behind that, under normal circumstances, it would have closed, forcing us to wait before opening again. Given the heads-up, the controller kept the bridge open for us as we watched car traffic back up on the bridge above. We sailed through without incident.

Long before we arrived at the bridge, we looked at both our paper charts and our chart plotter (you know, my boyfriend, Zeus) to check out our options and come up with a plan should we be forced to stop before passing under the bridge.

Harbortown Marina was new to us; we didn't know the setup or even where we would be docked. Since it could be tricky to get in and tied to the dock under sail alone, we opted to stop in the anchorage outside the marina. We anchored under sail and called TowBoatUS to bring us in. Purists will tell you we absolutely could have sailed in. But there were so many unknown variables that we did not deem it prudent to attempt. Besides, we paid for a TowBoatUS membership; we thought we might as well use it before heading out of the country. Once we were safely at anchor, we made three calls: TowBoatUS, the marina, and Tanya.

The *Take Two* gang had lived on and off at Harbortown for five years. Tanya is incredibly friendly, and she is not above using bribery, including baked goods and well-behaved children, to cement loyal friendships. Moreover, she is a force of nature. So, it came as no surprise when, at the height of the busy season for marinas in Florida, we were directed onto an ideally positioned dock right behind *Take Two*. Much like in DC, we became dock neighbors once again.

Michael went in search of *Take Two's* mechanic, Ben; Ally and Sarah picked up right where they left off two months before and could be found coloring mandalas, playing jacks or Mancala, practicing handstands and cartwheels or baking divine treats together, like the famous Hackney Brownies.

Tanya and I also picked up right where we left off. Over tea one afternoon, she gave me the entire scoop for the Exumas in the Bahamas. She even sent us along with their old cruising guide, *The Exuma Guide: A Cruising Guide to the Exuma Cays,* by Stephen Pavlidis. While she talked, I took copious notes on everything she said, including their favorite stops, where to find provisions, ideal locations to anchor, and great places to kayak. I soaked up every bit of Tanya's "local knowledge," which we later used.

Our new mechanic, Ben, alongside his capable apprentice, thirteen-year-old Aaron of *Take Two*, set out to diagnose *Ally Cat's* engine issue. The conclusion? The brackets meant to secure the heat exchanger were either not sufficiently tightened or had loosened over time, leading to friction and subsequent wear. The heat exchanger was worn through and needed to be replaced. The heat exchanger, an expensive part which cost in the neighborhood of $1,000, sadly was not included in our spare parts inventory, as this really wasn't a foreseeable situation.

Ben immediately got on the phone to find a replacement. In short order, he came up with both a new part and a refurbished one, which was about half the cost. Conferring with Michael and Jay, *Take Two's* captain, the decision was made to go for the refurbished part. Ben ordered it and had it shipped—unfortunately, not by next-day air.

With Christmas fast approaching, the "girls" from *Take Two* and *Ally Cat* planned a very special night. We had tickets to see *The Nutcracker* at the beautiful historic Sunrise Theater in Ft. Pierce. The downtown area was handsomely decked out, as were we. What fun we had! I am pretty sure Rachel, Tanya's youngest, did not stop dancing for well over a week.

After reveling in *The Nutcracker*, we were all in the Christmas spirit. Even though it was nearly 80 degrees, we decorated the boat. While packing up our decorations after Christmas in 2013, I kept out a few things to help make Christmas on *Ally Cat* feel more like home during the holidays. Tucked away in my holiday bin were all three of our stockings, which we hung with suction cup hooks near the galley, and about twenty ornaments. Since a traditional tree was out of the question, we used suction cup hooks to hang our ornaments around the salon, as well.

Weeks before, in Wilmington, North Carolina, I found an enormous pine cone during a run in the rain. It filled me with such joy that I carried it all the way back to *Ally Cat* to show Michael and Ally. As it dried in the cockpit, it began to open up, resembling a small tree. A thought occurred to me: "A little tree! We can decorate it and use it as our Christmas tree."

Ally and Sarah had a great time with this project. We visited the craft stores in Vero Beach for ideas on how to mount our tree and decorate it. It's remarkable what two resourceful girls armed with a glue gun can create! They even found miniature presents to place under their precious tree. But what about snow? Ally remembered seeing popcorn used as "snow" for decorating gingerbread houses in previous years; however, they were concerned that in the hot, humid climate, popcorn might become soggy and fall off. Cotton balls, on the other hand, were perfect.

While Sarah and Ally went small, creating the ideal tiny tree to decorate *Ally Cat*, *Take Two* definitely opted for grand in their outdoor decorations. Eli, their oldest, shimmied up and down their sixty-five-foot mast, fashioning strands of green lights into the shape of a tree. We all stared in wonder later that evening when it was illuminated. And Michael and

I enjoyed it out of the window in our berth every night before we went to bed.

Michael found 12-volt white Christmas light strands, which created quite a festive atmosphere in our cockpit. In fact, I loved them *so* much that after the holidays, I took to calling them our "party lights," and they stayed up the entire trip.

Since it was just the three of us on *Ally Cat*, most nights we joined the Hackneys for dinner aboard the much roomier forty-eight-foot *Take Two*. We always contributed in some way to the dinner, and I helped Tanya with both prep and cleanup, though I suppose when you regularly cook for seven, adding three more is not really a big deal. Before we headed to the Bahamas and the *Take Two* left for Naples to celebrate Christmas with family, I wanted to have them all over to *Ally Cat* for dinner, so I invited them for Christmas Eve.

"Are you *sure*?" Tanya asked incredulously. "We *never* get invited *anywhere* for dinner as a family!" Convinced I was serious, we set a time. Of course, I had to borrow her commercial-sized pressure cooker to make the *vat* of chicken tortilla soup since I tripled the recipe we normally used. And they had to bring their own bowls and spoons to supplement our supply. Though our girl had never hosted so many for dinner, we all fit just fine and had a grand evening.

Unable to convince *Take Two* to go to the Bahamas with us (they gave us some flimsy excuse about safety-related repairs), amidst sad so-longs, we promised to meet in the Bahamas in the spring of 2016, when we would be heading north on our way home and they would finally be heading south, on their way to Grenada.

The heat exchanger. Whatever happened with the heat exchanger? That is a longer story than it needed to be, albeit one with a happy ending.

The refurbished part arrived *ten* days after Ben ordered it due to a combination of the standard delivery he selected and holiday mail delays. And it was the wrong part. It was the Friday before Christmas, and Michael was so frustrated that he took to the phone and internet and found the part himself—a new part, so full-priced—and had it sent via next-day air. On Monday, when the part arrived, Michael eagerly opened the box, only to discover it, too, was the wrong part.

Ben and Aaron, and an incredibly exasperated Michael, sat down with the old part, the new part, our hard copy of the Westerbeke manual, and an online version of the manual to figure out what was going on. Oddly, the new part we received had the same number as the old part. However, the part did not match the picture in either manual, which was the same in both manuals, nor did it look like the old part. And it sure as heck would not fit in *Ally Cat's* engine.

At the time, I didn't grasp what a big deal this was for Michael. After all, we planned to stop in Ft. Pierce for at least a week to do final provisioning, and were having a ton of fun. It was not until he described *Ally Cat* as not being "whole" that I started to understand his anguish. Living on a sailboat, particularly once you leave the United States, is an adventure in self-sufficiency. We learned to make many of the foods we ate from scratch with basic ingredients, we made our own electricity via the sun, and we even made our own potable water with our onboard reverse osmosis water maker. Michael knew every system on board intimately, and he could maintain them all, as he had either installed or replaced every one. And now *Ally Cat* was disabled, and he was not able to fix her.

After numerous phone calls, Michael finally located the part.

"Can you please take it out of the box and send us a picture? And can I send you a picture so you can compare the part you are looking at with it?" Michael asked.

"Excuse me?" Once they realized the details of the part fiasco, they were more than happy to comply.

It was a miracle, a Christmas miracle: their part looked *exactly* like *Ally Cat's* broken part. "Can you put some wings on that heat exchanger and get it to Ft. Pierce as soon as possible?" Michael asked.

We have the best picture of Michael, visibly relieved, under the mistletoe in our cockpit, on Christmas Eve Day, kissing his brand new, bright Westerbeke red heat exchanger.

Next stop: No Name Harbor in Key Biscayne, not far from Miami. And then the Bahamas, where we rang in the new year.

'Twas the Night Before Christmas *Ally Cat* Style

'Twas the night before Christmas
  And the boat was alive
There was chaos and cornbread
  And chicken tortilla soup to be tried.

The stockings were hung
  By the galley with care
In hopes that St. Nicholas
  Would have a clue where we were.

The pinecone tree was glued
  To a small wooden block
And decorated with tiny ornaments
  And lights, all while sitting on the dock.

Their tree needed some snow
  Though none could be found
How about cotton balls?
  Be creative, just look around!

The sugar cookies were cut
  And baked on *Take Two*
Then decorated with sprinkles
  Of red and green. What? No blue?

The girls got all fancy
  And went out for a show
It was finally time
  To see *The Nutcracker*, you know.

Once *Ally Cat's* engine was running again
  It was sad
But it was time
  To say, "so long" to our friends.

With hopes of meeting
  In the Bahamas the next year
Somehow we left
  Without shedding too many tears.

The mistletoe was hung
  In the cockpit, oh my
Apparently, I'll do anything to score a kiss
  From my sweetie pie!

Santa did find us in Florida
  We were not to be missed
Presents were thoughtful but few
  And a bright red heat exchanger topped the list!

*"I learned that courage is not the absence of fear, but
the triumph over it. The brave man is not he who does
not feel afraid, but he who conquers that fear."*
—*Nelson Mandela*

EPILOGUE

THE BAHAMAS AND BEYOND

"You can. You should. And if you are brave enough to start, you will." —Stephen King

Once we left Florida for the Bahamas at the end of December 2014, *Ally Cat* did not return to the United States for the next eighteen months. Michael, Ally, and I traveled to Massachusetts for a few weeks in the summer of 2015 to visit relatives and friends and get our teeth cleaned.

Although I filled pages and pages of journal entries while I was traveling, my words were often not filtered enough to share. Sometime before our first RV trip in 2004, I learned the neatest trick. In addition to the decidedly low-tech solution of writing in a small page-per-month calendar to remember where we have been, when, and with whom, I started sending postcards home to us. The calendar provided a concise overview of our itinerary, while each postcard, signed "Love Us," captured a snapshot, including our thoughts and emotions, from the places we visited.

Starting when we left Massachusetts in August 2014 and continuing until we returned home two years later, I did the same with our sailing adventure. Sometimes, particularly at the beginning of our trip, we were able to buy postcards representing the landmarks we visited and the places we saw. Later, say in the Out Islands of the Bahamas, when there was not even a store in which to buy a postcard, Ally and I got creative and made our own.

As we sailed through the Bahamas to Turks and Caicos and the Dominican Republic, then south of Puerto Rico and the Virgin Islands into the Eastern Caribbean, and all the way to Grenada and back home to Massachusetts, we chronicled our journey in these postcards. Imagine my surprise when, two years later, I discovered there were more than three hundred of them!

I finally decided to launch a blog, *Love Us: Postcards from the Crew of Three,* on my website https://kimberlyjwardwriter.com/blog/, to both preserve and share them. If you want more of our story, please check out my blog!

I introduced the idea of "reentry" in Chapter 5 in terms of the money we would need to get reestablished once we returned home. It's not hard to grasp the tangible things we needed to get set up again, such as cell phones, a car, and a bike for Ally, not to mention a whole new winter wardrobe since she grew eight inches in two years.

Much more difficult to explain is what it's like to return home to our old lives as wholly changed people. We may have seemed much the same, but we were *different.* We not only had passport stamps for each of the sixteen different countries we sailed to, but we also met the people, ate their food, and learned how they lived. And it left an indelible impression on each of us. As Oliver Wendell Holmes said, "A mind that is stretched by a new experience can never go back to its old dimensions."

Before we left, I said to Michael, "If we can send Ally to junior high with the confidence to march to her own drum, our trip will have been a success."

Ally started seventh grade just a few weeks after we moved back into our old house. While everything about junior high was incredibly noisy and busy compared to living on a boat, Ally eventually settled in and thrived. By Spring Break, she even decided to join a small group of students traveling to the Netherlands, Germany, and Poland on a "Holocaust Tour" with two of her favorite teachers, including Mr. Orie (Remember the phenomenal teacher who finally got Ally writing?). One of just a handful of seventh graders, she was confident enough to sign up and skilled enough to pack completely on her own. As Robin Lee Graham, who set out to sail around the world alone as a teenager in 1965, said, "At sea, I learned how little a person needs, not how much." Graham, author of *Dove,* about his journeys as the youngest person to sail around the world alone, also said, "Life would be pretty monotonous if the sky was always blue."

Two years later, as a freshman in high school, Ally opted to travel again, this time with her English teacher and a group of juniors and seniors, to England and Scotland. Having personally experienced studying abroad in the United Kingdom three decades before, I eagerly followed her travels by way of a phone app. One morning, to my utter surprise, her name lit up my caller ID. Generally, since moving off the boat, she communicated with us via text messages rather than engaging in actual phone conversations.

"Mom, I found where I belong! I found my people."

Quickly checking out her location, I noticed she was right next to the University of Edinburgh in Scotland! Uh oh.

Though she was only in Scotland for a mere thirty hours, fourteen-year-old Ally was convinced she wanted to go to university there. She intended to go on another school trip, to Ireland and Scotland, in April 2020, as she wisely said she wanted to see if her obsession with Scotland was actually true love or simply an infatuation. However, the COVID-19 pandemic started, disrupting everything.

Though *nothing* was normal about college planning in 2020 and 2021, we did manage to squeeze in a six-day whirlwind *mission* to visit five universities in Scotland. And it was true love. Even Michael and I could see that.

As I finish this postscript, Ally has just returned home to Massachusetts for the summer after completing her first year at the University of Glasgow. She is studying molecular and cellular biology (MCB) and *loves* Scotland! I had to look up what MCB was, and I am finally convinced we did not ruin her by boatschooling for fifth and sixth grades.

Before leaving Scotland, she and a roommate moved into a flat, where she is likely to live until she finishes her under-graduate studies. Sadly, this may be her last summer living at home with us. Apparently, when you breed a traveler, she travels.

Roots and wings. I have long said those are the two best gifts we give our children.

Michael seemingly did not miss a beat as a technical consultant, and exactly one week after we moved off *Ally Cat*, he was back in the office. Amusingly, not a single one of his coworkers had any idea where he had been the past two years. And they had *no* idea he was desperately trying to shake out the cobwebs, not to mention get used to wearing long pants and shoes all day.

Having pushed retirement back at least five years by taking our sabbatical, Michael planned to consult for ten more years after we returned, which would get Ally through junior high and high school plus four years of university. After his first week of consulting with his new client in Cleveland, Ohio, Michael and I were out for a walk. I can still remember the exact spot on the marsh where he stopped and said, "I don't know if I can do this for ten more years."

I understood completely. "Okay, what else do you want to do?" Remember, always have a Plan B. And C and D.

He looked out over our cove, home to our neighbor's oyster farm, and said, "I think I'll volunteer my time with Bob this fall to see if I might like oyster farming."

"And I am going to write," I added. I always knew I had a book in me. After living on a sailboat for two years, I knew I finally had just the story to tell, too. While Michael was traveling that week, I signed up for a memoir writing course at the local library. Many of the words I wrote in my first few essays are the basis for the chapters you just read.

In the winter of 2017, Michael and I discussed our business plan for an oyster farm. The conversations and planning were not dissimilar to those we had when planning to go sailing, except this time, everything was new to both of us!

True to their nature, you can make plans, but you can't plan the outcome. As the summer of 2018 rolled around, once the lengthy permitting process was complete, we were up to our chins in oyster equipment and baby oysters. I was slowly moving ahead with my manuscript, and Michael was still consulting full-time, when my mother experienced a series of crises in Colorado, resulting in her move to Massachusetts. After some major renovations to our house to make it accessible, she eventually moved in with us.

Four years and a lifetime of COVID later, she is much healthier and living on her own in an assisted living community twenty minutes away. Mattapoisett Oysters, which often feels like a massive science experiment, not to mention an exercise in stamina, is finally showing a profit, no thanks to a global pandemic. Michael continued consulting until March 2021, when he gleefully gave his notice. I made the mistake of saying he was "retired," which did not go over too well with him. He has a point, as neither of us has ever worked so hard!

After unexpectedly becoming a full-time in-home caregiver all through Ally's high school years, during a pandemic, I somehow forgot who that fierce gal was who went sailing so far out of her comfort zone. I felt as if not only had I lost my writing voice, but I had also lost myself. No matter what I tried, I couldn't excavate my authentic soul.

Finally, in 2023, I committed to taking as good care of myself as I have always done for those I love. After a mindset and attitude readjustment, I dusted off my rough draft and finished it, then revised it. After hiring a professional editor and finalizing my manuscript, I hired a publishing service provider to learn the skills I needed to publish *Crew of Three: How Bold Dreams and Detailed Plans Launched Our Family's Sailing Adventure* with my very own company, KJW Publishing. And I have many more stories to tell.

What about *Ally Cat*? Not to worry. She's still very much part of our family, along with the completely crazy coonhound Tori that we rescued in 2018. *Ally Cat* went in the water in 2017, the year after we returned home, before all the permits were complete, to start up our oyster venture. As you can imagine, with all we had going on the next four years, she did not go in the water and was virtually neglected on her stands in our side yard. In 2022, before heading to university, Ally wanted to take one more vacation on the boat, so we got her ready and launched her. After a delightful week on Martha's Vineyard, where Michael and I caught COVID, she proved to be the perfect quarantine hotel as well!

As *Crew of Three* heads to press, we are again preparing to take *Ally Cat* cruising. Our plans are to sail to the Bahamas from January through March 2024 and each year after until it no longer amuses us. Stay tuned to see how God laughs at that plan.

"You can choose courage or comfort, but you cannot choose both." —Brené Brown

THANK YOU FOR READING MY BOOK

Reviews are critical to authors. I appreciate your feedback, and I love hearing what you have to say. My goal is to constantly grow as a writer, and I am committed to making each book better than the last.

Please take a few minutes to leave a review on Amazon, or your preferred retailer, letting me know what you thought of the book.

You can also leave a review on Goodreads and BookBub.

Do you want more of our story?

I have launched my blog, where you can see and read the more than three hundred postcards we sent home from our adventures, plus many more photos and stories.

https://kimberlyjwardwriter.com/blog/

I'd love to hear from you! Please feel free to be in touch via social media.

Facebook Kimberly J. Ward, Writer

https://www.facebook.com/KimberlyJWardWriter/

Instagram @KimberlyJWardWriter

https://www.instagram.com/kimberlyjwardwriter/

DOWNLOAD THE AUDIOBOOK FREE

As a way to thank you for purchasing this paperback
or eBook, I am giving you the audiobook version
of *Crew of Three: How Bold Dreams and Detailed Plans
Launched Our Family's Sailing Adventures* at no cost.

I even narrated it myself!

Please visit my website to get your free gift:

www.KimberlyJWardWriter.com/Audiobook

ACKNOWLEDGMENTS

My friend and fellow author Tanya Hackney told me that finishing the rough draft was akin to giving birth. I still had to raise it from infancy to adulthood. It takes a village, and I am grateful you are in mine.

Andrea Marcovici, from the time our children were babies and my book was a newborn until both reached adulthood, you have been unwavering in your support and editing insight. I could not have done any of it without you.

My fellow cruiser and writer Mary Connaughton, thank you for getting me writing again when I was stuck. Your friendship means the world to me.

I am grateful for my multitalented friend Cherí Ben-Iesau— author, artist, and farmer—for creating the perfect motif for my Crew of Three.

I believe what is meant for me always arrives on time. Rhonda Douglas's *Book Finishers Bootcamp* was exactly what I needed to finish my book. Thank you for sharing your wisdom, particularly regarding mindset.

I am eternally grateful for my talented editor Howard Lovy. Thank you for your skills and kindness in helping me to write the best story I knew how. You helped me raise my book from an angsty teen to a mature adult.

And last, though definitely not least, I am thankful every day for the privilege of walking through this life with Michael and Ally, my two favorite people in the world. Thank you for your unconditional love, unending support, and ability to make me laugh. Always.

APPENDIX A

CHARTS AND GUIDES

Navionics electronic charts for North and South America

Maptech Chartbook Nantucket to New York (including New Jersey)

Maptech Chartbook Chesapeake and Delaware Bays

Maptech Chartbook Norfolk to FL

Maptech Chartbook FL East Coast

On the Water CruiseGuide for the Intracoastal Waterway (ICW) (Mark and Diana Doyle)

Bahamas (Insight Pocket Guide)

Fodor's Bahamas (Fodor Travel)

MustSees Bahamas (Michelin)

C-Map Explorer electronic charts for the Bahamas

Explorer Chart Bimini Islands and the Crossings of The Straits of Florida

Explorer Chartbook Near Bahamas (Monty and Sara Lewis)

Explorer Chartbook Exumas and Ragged Islands (Monty and Sara Lewis)

The Exuma Guide: A Cruising Guide to the Exuma Cays (Stephen J. Pavlidis)

A Cruising Guide to the Southern Bahamas (Stephen J. Pavlidis)

The Caribbean Like A Local (Michelin)

Caribbean (Eyewitness Travel)

The Gentleman's Guide to Passages South: The Thornless Path to Windward (Bruce Van Sant)

A Cruising Guide to Puerto Rico (Stephen J. Pavlidis)

The Cruising Guide to the Virgin Islands (Nancy & Simon Scott)

The Cruising Guide to the Leeward Islands: Anguilla through Dominica (Chris Doyle)

Sailors Guide to the Winward Islands: Martinique to Grenada (Chris Doyle)

APPENDIX B

REFERENCE BOOKS

Eldridge Tide and Pilot Book 2014

Eldridge Tide and Pilot Book 2016

Marine Medicine (Eric Weiss, MD and Michael E. Jacobs, MD)

Sailing Skills and Seamanship (USCG Auxiliary)

Sailboat Maintenance Manual (Don Casey's)

Coastal and Offshore Weather: The Essential Handbook (Chris Parker, s/v Bel Ami)

The Cruiser's Handbook of Fishing (Scott Bannerot and Wendy Bannerot)

Children's World Atlas (DK Publishing)

The World (Michelin)

Flags of the World Flash Cards (Dalmatian Press)

Almanac of World Facts (Rand McNally)

Pure Sea Glass Identification Deck (Richard LaMotte)

Birds of the West Indies (Princeton University Press)

Birds of the Eastern Caribbean (Peter Evans)

Reef Coral Identification: Florida, Caribbean, Bahamas (Paul Humann, Ned DeLoach)

Reef Fish Identification: Florida, Caribbean, Bahamas (Paul Humann, Ned DeLoach)

Reef Creature Identification: Florida, Caribbean, Bahamas (Paul Humann, Ned DeLoach)

Snorkeling Guide to Marine Life: Florida, Caribbean, Bahamas (Paul Humann, Ned DeLoach)

The Shell Book: Atlantic, Gulf and Caribbean (Sandra Romashko)

The Boat Galley Cookbook (Carolyn Sherlock and Jan Irons)

The Care and Feeding of Sailing Crew (Lin Pardey)

Easy Vegetarian Cooking (Sharon Cadwallader)

How to Cook Everything: The Basics (Mark Bittman)

New Recipes from Moosewood Restaurant (Moosewood Collective Staff)

Pain Free (Pete Egoscue)

APPENDIX C

HOMESCHOOL NOTICE OF INTENT

Fifth Grade

August 17, 2014

Dear Dr. White,

I am writing regarding our plans for our daughter's schooling for the next two years. Our daughter, Allison Ward, completed the fourth grade at Old Hammondtown School during the 2013-14 year. Just prior to the start of the 2014-15 school year, we are planning to depart for a two-year adventure as liveaboards on our sailboat, s/v *Ally Cat*.

We—Ally's dad, Michael, Ally and I—will be leaving MA and sailing down to the Washington, DC-area, where we will stay for about 6-8 weeks. The first week of November, we will again head South, along the Intercoastal Waterway (ICW), down to the Miami area. From there, we will provision for about a four-month stay in the Bahamas.

Somewhere around February or March, 2015, we will head to Turks and Caicos and into the Eastern Caribbean—through Dominican Republic, Puerto Rico, the Virgin Islands, the Leeward Islands, the Windward Islands, and finally down to Grenada, where we will wait out the hurricane season (approximately July through November 2015).

After all danger of hurricanes has passed, we will basically retrace our steps—or stop at any of the places we might have missed on the way down!—and make our way back home.

During this time, my husband and I will be Ally's primary teachers. Based in large part on the experiences we will have, along with a structured curriculum, we plan to homeschool, or rather boatschool, Ally for fifth and sixth grades.

To get a better benchmark to determine where I needed to start, I gave Ally the fourth grade California Achievement Test (CAT Level 14), via Seton Testing Services, in May 2014. She did very well, so I gave her the fifth grade test (CAT Level 15) in July 2105, where she scored almost identically as she did on the Level 14. I have enclosed copies of these test results.

Our planned school year will start Monday, September 8, 2014. We will school for 36 weeks, five days a week, until July

3, 2015, taking 7 weeks off. Our plan is to work for 5 hours a day, divided between coursework and experiential learning.

I have spent a considerable amount of time researching what Ally would be and should be learning. Last fall, I was given a copy of the 2011 MA Frameworks for Math and ELA. I have also spent time on the DESE site becoming familiar with the resources there. In conversation with both classroom teachers, as well as homeschool parents, I was pointed in the direction of The Core Knowledge Sequence, which provided me with content and skill guidelines, by grade, in a concise easy-for-me-to-read format. What Your Fifth Grader Needs to Know (Hirsh) expanded on the sequence. What follows is our interpretation of what we think *our* fifth grader needs to know.

We will cover the following area:

1. Math

2. Science

3. English

4. Social Studies

5. Geography

6. Computers & Technology

7. Foreign Language

8. Music

9. Art

10. Physical Education

Math

We will be going through the Pearson-Scott Forseman Mathematics textbook for grade 5, as well as the supplemental workbook. Additional resources that we will use include: Writing in Mathematics (Globe Fearon), two Problem Solving workbooks (Heath Mathematics), and Understanding Fractions, Decimals & Percents workbook (Pearson-Prentice Hall). If further resources are necessary, we will consult Khan Academy.

Science

We will be going through the Pearson-Scott Foresman Science textbook, which includes the following sections: Life Science, Earth Science, Physical Science and Space and Technology. We will utilize the Focus on Science workbook as a companion to the text.

Power is a very big deal aboard a sailboat. Having enough electricity when and where you need it is critical. We have installed a solar panel to meet our needs, with the necessary components to have both 110 and 12 volt options. We have included a unit study on Electricity, as Ally will be helping to monitor what has been produced and used aboard *Ally Cat* on a daily basis.

Weather is also integral to life on a boat. Though we have a general itinerary, all passage decisions will be made based on the weather, not on any schedule. In addition to listening to the weather multiple times a day and reading synopsis put together by experts, we will all be learning from the book, *Coastal and Offshore Weather – the Essential Handbook* (Chris Parker).

We are all nature lovers and are keen to explore via walking, hiking, kayaking, snorkeling, stand-up paddle boarding, and maybe even snuba! Some of the beautifully illustrated books that made the cut to come aboard are: *Reef Coral Identification*, *Reef Creature Identification*, and *Reef Fish Identification* (Humann and Delaoch), *Nature of the Islands* (Barlow), *Birds of the Eastern Caribbean* (Evans) and *The Shell Book* (Romashko).

English

Ally LOVES to read; we all do! We have Kindle readers *loaded* with tons of books—from *Little House on the Prairie* to *Harry Potter*, *Nancy Drew* to *The Secret Garden*, historical fiction, cookbooks, biographies, gardening how to's, novels, textbooks, and just about everything in between. Thank goodness this technology is available so we are able to take all the reading material we want, as well as to be able to update and add to it along the way!

Mechanics appears to be the area where Ally needs emphasis; therefore, we have included the following resources: *The Complete Book of Grammar and Punctuation* (American Education), *Checking Your Grammar* (Terban), and *Grammar and Writing Practice Book* (Pearson-Scott Forseman).

In an effort to keep Ally writing, she will be responsible for regular updates to our (yet-to-be- determined) blog site (see Computers!). We will give her assignments based on our location and activities. We will also be utilizing *The Writers Solution* (Prentice Hall) to continue to develop various writing styles.

Additionally, we will use the *SourceBank Workbook* for Grade 6 (Silver Burdett Ginn) to supplement Ally's reading and writing.

Social Studies

We will be reading the five books in the Our America series (Kilbride) to get back into the swing of school: *The Pilgrim Adventure, The King Phillips War Adventure, The Salem Adventure, The Revolutionary Way Adventure,* and *The Pioneer Adventure.* Each of the books in this time-traveling-twins adventure series has accompanying activities, as well.

The Civil and Revolutionary Wars will be the main focus during our stay in DC. We will be able to incorporate many relevant field trips into our schooling, including Appomattox, Bull Run, Frederick Douglass' home, and possibly even Gettysburg. Without question, we will be able to read the Gettysburg Address from the granite walls of the Jefferson Memorial!

We will be following The Civil War Curriculum, designed by the Civil War Trust. Additionally, Ally will read *The Road to Freedom 1815-1900* (McCague) as well as the *Narrative of the Life of Frederick Douglass: An American Slave* (by Frederick Douglass). We have also included the locally produced document, *African Americans, Abolitionism and New Bedford.*

As we delve into the Revolutionary War, we will use *Celebrate America* (Hellriegel) as our guide, and are planning visits to Mount Vernon, Monticello and the White House, if we can arrange it. We will learn more about each President by studying *US Presidents* (Green), as well as visiting each of the presidential memorials.

Cases and Controversies in US History (Walch and O'Halloran) should provide material for thought-provoking discussions. Perhaps we can take 'sides' and research enough to have our own debate.

To supplement the above, we will use *World History: Telescoping the Times* (McDougal Littell), as well as unit studies covering the Late 1800's, 1900-1039 and 1940-1965.

Geography

Since we will be arriving in every port by boat, public transport will be our transportation of choice! In DC, Ally will learn how to navigate the Metro system, as well as the extensive network of bus transportation, so we can explore further than our feet can take us.

As we are a family who travels regularly, her map skills are fairly advanced, however, she will be adding charts and coastal navigation to her skill set, as well. Both her father and I are US Coast Guard-trained navigators and are able to determine where we are and get where we are going without the assistance of electronics, though we hope not to be in that particular situation! By the time we return to MA, Ally should be proficient in these skills, as well.

Computers and Technology

Ally's father and I are both computer consultants and very comfortable with and adept on computers. With various writing assignments, we will require presentations in a variety of formats, as well, to continue to hone her skills with Word, PowerPoint and Excel. We may even try our hand at giving and receiving assignments via Google Docs!

One of our first computer assignments will be to research where to set up our blog. Ally will design the layout and will be responsible for posting much of the content through daily writing activities. We are also hopeful that we will produce some of our own videos using video taken with our GoPro camera and edited on the computer.

We will not have cell phones once we leave the US, and we will not always have access to the internet. We are estimating that we may have it a third to half of the time. There are many options available to stay connected. Ally will work with us to help determine what our needs are, as well as how to best meet them, given the available options.

We will be using Skype as the primary method to 'talk' with family and friends. Ally will help design a training manual for her Grandmother to learn the ins and outs of using Skype—and perhaps even Facebook!

In addition to continued mastery of the internet and PC applications, Ally will also be learning about the electronics that are used to run the boat: chart plotter, GPS, depth sounder and radar.

Foreign Language

Ally participated in the French Club with Mrs. Cassi last spring. Though French would benefit us in many parts of the Caribbean we will be visiting, my rusty high-school and college Spanish has won out for teaching. We will be following the *Spanish Every Day* (Harvey) workbook and CDs at the suggestions of several Spanish teachers.

Music

Ally started playing the flute last year with Mrs. Lafleur and loved it! Mrs. Lafleur sent her home at the end of the year with some music and the title of the next practice book, *Tradition of Excellence, Book 2* (Pearson and Nowlin). Her flute and music will both accompany us on our trip and regular practice times will be established within our school day. Concerts for all in ear-shot!

Art

We have brought some art supplies with us—colored pencils, markers, and crayons, stamps, glue, etc.—and will see where our creativity and nature's bounty take us. Ally has recently learned to crochet, as well. We have some hooks and yarn packed on board, too.

Our first art project, however, will be to design our 'boat cards.' Once we have set up our blog and have an address, we will design a calling card with a logo and our contact information, as we will be meeting many new people all along our journey.

Physical Education

Our day is likely to begin with some sort of activity, as this is important to all of us! In DC, there will be lots of walking and scooter-riding. As we make our way to warmer weather, we will take to the water: swimming, kayaking, and stand-up paddle boarding.

And it promises to be an interesting time, with the onset of puberty! We have had a number of conversations about what is happening in her body and the bodies of those around her. I will be in touch with Ms. Balsis, who hopefully can provide the link for the Human Sexuality video that Ally's classmate will be seeing this year, as well.

We are thrilled to have this opportunity and are very dedicated to Ally's education. If you have any questions about our plans, please do not hesitate to contact us.

Thank you,

Kimberly and Michael Ward

Sixth Grade

September 5, 2015

Dear Dr. White,

   I am writing to update you regarding our plans for our daughter's schooling during the second year of our two-year sailing trip. Our daughter, Allison Ward, completed the fifth grade aboard our sailboat, s/v Ally Cat, during the 2014-15 year.

   We—Ally's dad, Michael, Ally and I—left MA August 2014, sailing down to the Washington, DC-area, where we stayed for about 7 weeks. We then spent 3 weeks in Hampton, VA, before heading south, along the Intracoastal Waterway (ICW), down to the Miami area. Just after Christmas, we provisioned and headed to the Bahamas for three months.

   In March, 2015, we headed to Turks and Caicos and into the Eastern Caribbean—through the Dominican Republic, Puerto Rico, and the Virgin Islands. Making stops in St. Martin, Montserrat, Antigua, Dominica, Martinique, St. Lucia, and St. Vincent & the Grenadines. We are now in Grenada for the hurricane season. After all danger of hurricanes has passed, we will basically retrace our steps, stopping at any of the places we might have missed on the way down and stopping again at our favorites, making our way back to MA in August 2016.

   Again this year, my husband and I will be Ally's primary teachers. Based in large part on the experiences we will have, along with a structured curriculum, we plan to homeschool, or rather boatschool, Ally again for the sixth grade.

   In August 2015, at the conclusion of fifth grade, I gave Ally the sixth grade California Achievement Test (CAT Level 16), via Seton Testing Services. Her scores are attached, as is a portfolio of her work from fifth grade.

   Our school year will start Tuesday, September 8, 2015. We will school for 36 weeks, five days a week, until the end of June 2016, taking 7 weeks off. Our plan is to work for 5 hours a day, divided between coursework and experiential learning.

   We will cover the following area:

1. Math

2. Science

3. English and Language Arts

4. Social Studies

5. Geography

6. Spanish

7. Art and Music

8. Physical Education

Math

We will continue to use *Teaching Textbooks Math 6*. She is more than halfway through this curriculum, having completed the tests with a 98% average. We will move on to Math 7 when she completes 6.

Science

For 5th grade, we utilized the *Focus on Science Level E*, workbook. We will continue with the Level F workbook this year. We will also be using Ignite Science for middle school, which includes topics in Earth, Life and Physical sciences, as well as general science topics, such as the Scientific Method, Experimentation, Understanding Science, etc.

We have two science projects planned. The first is a volcano unit, which we have shared with a number of other 'kid boats.' After visiting so many islands that were formed as a result of volcanoes—and hiking UP a number of them!—this unit will be quite relevant. The project will culminate with the kids delivering powerpoint presentations and erupting their homemade volcanoes!

The second project will be on humpback whales. On our way south, we crossed paths in Turks & Caicos with the migrating humpback whales, heading north. It was simply majestic! We have decided to time our trip north to coincide with this phenomenon again, as well as to witness the mating and calving, much of which happens near Samaná, Dominican Republic.

English

We have selected three novels this year as 'school reading': *Where the Red Fern Grows* (Wilson Rawls), *The Cay* (Theodore Taylor), and *Anne of Green Gables* (Lucy Maud Montgomery). More structured this year, we have comprehension questions for each of the books, as well as a quiz.

Amazon gift cards are the gift of choice from family members while we are traveling. Any time we have a decent internet connection, we download more books! Getting Ally to read has never been a problem...getting her to go to sleep rather than read, is the problem!

Ally is working with 20 new vocabulary words every three weeks. The first week she writes each word on an index card, and completes KIMS on the back of the index card (**K**:Keyword; **I**:information/definition; **M**:memory device/ picture; and **S**: sentence using the word which demonstrates she understands the meaning) for 10 words. The second week she completes KIMS for the remaining 10 words. The last week she takes a spelling test and writes a vocabulary story. She started last year using 7 words in the story and increased each time until she was using 11 words in her story. We will keep adding an extra word until the stories become nonsensical!

Ally will continue to be responsible for regular updates to our www.CrewOfThree.com blog site. We will be working through *Checking Your Grammar and Getting It Right* (Marvin Terban) to continue to hone Ally's writing mechanics. Ally also writes a minimum of 3 postcards per week to friends and family.

Social Studies

For historical fiction, this year we will be reading the eight books from the Shadows from the Past series, by Wendy Leighton-Porter: *The Shadow of Atlantis, The Shadow of Minotaur, The Shadow of the Trojan Horse, The Shadow of the Pyramid, The*

Shadow of the Volcano, The Shadow of Camelot, The Shadow of the Norman Arrow, and *The Shadow of the Two Princes.*

We will also be using the Ignite Social Studies for middle school this year, which includes topics in MA State History, Early American History, World Cultures and World History.

Cases and Controversies in US History (Walch and O'Halloran) will continue to provide material for thought-provoking discussions. It has been interesting to take 'sides' and have our own debates. To supplement the above, we will also use *World History: Telescoping the Times* (McDougal Littell).

Geography

During the past year, visiting 15 different countries, Ally learned how to get around! Starting when we set off from Grenada (after hurricane season is deemed over according to the insurance companies), Ally will be learning *Sailing and Seamanship*, as well as *Coastal Navigation*, based on the US Coast Guard Auxiliary training materials.

Spanish

Having completed the book and CDs for *Spanish Every Day* (Harvey) twice last year, we will be moving on to the Michel Thomas Method this year.

Music

Ally has two new flute music books from which she will learn pieces this year: *Patriotic Melodies* (Jonathon Robbins) and *Easy Pop Melodies* (Hal Leonard)

Art

We will continue to plan various art projects throughout the year. Additionally, we will be reading through *Discovering Great Artists* (Kohl and Solga) and completing as many of the activities as are feasible on a boat!

Physical Education

Given the fact that Ally played volleyball 6 out of the past 6 days, staying active has definitely not been a problem! We regularly hike, walk, swim, kayak, paddleboard, sail, ride horses, snorkel and play volleyball.

Again, we are thrilled to have this opportunity and are very dedicated to Ally's education. If you have any questions about our plans, please do not hesitate to contact us.

Thank you,

Kimberly and Michael Ward

About the Author

Kimberly J. Ward is an avid traveler, having had the opportunity to travel as a family growing up and study abroad in England during college. She has camped her way across the country through the US national parks three times, taken an extended honeymoon sailing through Nova Scotia, and enjoyed the luxury of several cruise ship excursions, in addition to exploring new places any chance she gets. She also spent ten years traveling full-time as a technical consultant.

Though she has written thousands of pages of journals, both at home and while traveling, Crew of Three: How Bold Dreams and Detailed Plans Launched Our Family's Sailing Adventure, is her first published work.

An adventurer, gardener, and writer, she never dreamed she would live on a sailboat for two years and homeschool her daughter. She graduated with a BS in Marketing Management and a minor in English from Virginia Polytechnic Institute and State University in 1990.

Originally from northern Virginia, Kimberly lives and works out of her home on the coast of Massachusetts with her husband and her crazy coonhound. When she is not working on their oyster farm or gardening, she enjoys hiking, cycling, kayaking, and, of course, traveling.

www.KimberlyJWardWriter.com

Facebook Kimberly J. Ward, Writer

https://www.facebook.com/KimberlyJWardWriter/

Instagram @KimberlyJWardWriter

https://www.instagram.com/kimberlyjwardwriter/

Printed in the USA
CPSIA information can be obtained
at www.ICGtesting.com
LVHW040344190324
774874LV00022B/252

9 798891 091023